ENGLISH LEARNERS AT HOME AND AT SCHOOL

ENGLISH LEARNERS AT HOME AND AT SCHOOL

Stories and Strategies

JOYCE W. NUTTA

Harvard Education Press
Cambridge, Massachusetts

Paperback ISBN 978-1-68253-690-2

Library of Congress Cataloging-in-Publication Data is on file.

Published by Harvard Education Press,
an imprint of the Harvard Education Publishing Group
Harvard Education Press
8 Story Street
Cambridge, MA 02138

Cover Design: Wilcox Design
Cover Image: calvindexter/DigitalVision Vectors via Getty Images

The typefaces in this book are Minion Pro and Myriad Pro.

Dedication: To Junné, the gift of our family's immigration story

CONTENTS

FOREWORD

POPULAR MEDIA are reporting that over the past three decades, around *30 million people* have immigrated to the United States, many with families that have included children, children who bring unique social and emotional needs, lack English language ability, have parents who cannot communicate in English, and the list goes on. But there is one thing that is in our favor—all parents, wherever they come from, want success for their children and have hope that school will make the lives of their kids safe, productive, and socially viable. That puts a heavy burden on you, the teacher, as you are likely to have a child in your classroom who has been separated from their parents at the border or comes with the emotional trauma of having lived in a war-torn country. So, helping these students gain the skills to be productive and socially competent means addressing the needs of the whole child . . . understanding the larger ecosystem, the environment that impacts their lives and shapes their ability to learn. That is asking a lot of today's teachers.

Having spent the past fifteen years in higher education administration, I am often asked, "Do you miss being in the classroom? Did you enjoy teaching and when did you know you were really reaching your students?" The easy answer is, "Once a teacher, always a teacher," and despite the "reforms" and political and policy environments that so complicate teaching today, it is nevertheless a profession I miss and deeply respect. That is why I am so pleased to write the foreword to this book.

As the president of Texas Woman's University, a majority-minority and Hispanic-serving institution (many having been English learner—EL—students), I see the end products of our K–12 education system every day, and I am always amazed to hear the stories of those students who came from incredibly challenging backgrounds. They often credit that very special teacher who gave them the inspiration to lift themselves up and *want* to become productive and independent citizens of our country. So, I am grateful to all of you who are reading this book and making an effort to strengthen your practice. Your efforts can help lift up those students who come your way.

Learning to teach effectively in today's multilingual classrooms is required of teachers at every grade level—from early elementary all the way through secondary. We have so many contributors who have been in these classrooms and who aim to impart their skills and knowledge to improving our profession; but, in this book, Dr. Joyce Nutta uses a technique that I believe is brilliant. She uses stories that are based in reality.

The power of stories is dramatic, but to be so, they must be relevant, recallable, and motivational, especially when used to improve professional practice. Steve Jobs told stories that made disciples out of his customers. Oprah Winfrey tells stories that her viewers never forget. That is what I love about this book and its powerful stories. One of the stories made me recall a time when I was leading a professional development session with rural teachers and how spending time listening to each individual's lived experience motivated the entire class to engage, embrace the topic, and relate at a much deeper level. And the stories in this book are not just about the didactic relationship between teacher and student. The relationship is much more dramatic than that today because it is an all-encompassing relationship that includes other students, the student's family, school administrators, and even the community where they live.

I am also inspired by this book because of Nutta's personal pathway into teaching and her commitment to the profession. Perhaps it was because as a teenager, Nutta was a second-language learner herself when her family moved to Italy. Also, her early teaching experience came out of an adult education background. That gave her special and unique insights into the needs of learners at many different levels. She became one of my doctoral students at the University of South Florida and had such passion for the requirements of effective EL teaching that we convinced her to join the faculty and help address our huge need in Florida. The state had just placed dramatic new demands on every teacher to acquire new EL skills via ongoing professional development. With her background, Nutta became a real leader in developing an effective professional development protocol to address this need.

Fortunately, today there are far more multilingual teachers than ever before, but a second-language ability only addresses a limited aspect of creating an effective classwide learning environment with students who might speak several different native languages. The ability to quickly assess speaking and writing abilities and to be sensitive to different cultures are required during the limited time teachers are trying to get to know their students. This sounds daunting, doesn't it? Just read "Dibenesha's Story." It is a great reminder to me of how difficult and important—but rewarding—this work is.

In her many years as a practitioner and academic researcher, Nutta has carefully identified key strategies that can be employed to make the classroom experience effective, but it is her deep understanding of what life is really like for these students, their families, and teachers as told through six compelling stories that make this such an important and meaningful book. The book also prompts excellent discussion to further develop the instructional tools that need to be understood and practiced.

As an academic and former teacher still committed to the powerful mission of teaching ELs, I am so grateful to Nutta for her continuing research in this field and for her efforts to curate such powerful stories and produce this book. It is a wonderful teaching tool and so representative of the actual challenges that both novice and veteran teachers face every day. We are fortunate to have it in our repertoire of high-quality teacher professional development literature.

Carine M. Feyten, PhD
President and Chancellor
Texas Woman's University

INTRODUCTION

THIS BOOK HAS A SIMPLE PREMISE. If teachers know, *really* know, their students, they are more able to help them succeed. Every teacher should know something about all their students, but many students come from families whose stories have less in common with the families of their teachers. My hope is that this book will provide insights into the struggles and triumphs of English learners and their families, so you will have a foundation on which to build a personal understanding of each individual English learner (EL) that you're lucky enough to have in your classroom.

ELs typically come from homes or places where English is not the primary language, and they have not yet attained full proficiency in English listening, speaking, reading, or writing, which affects their achievement in school. Although, as a group, ELs are defined by their developing English proficiency, there is as much diversity among ELs as there is between ELs and students who grew up speaking English. In other words, ELs are from all races, ethnicities, socioeconomic levels, educational backgrounds, and family compositions, with the same range of abilities and disabilities that non-EL students possess.[1]

If there is one lived experience, however, that most ELs have in common, it is their family's desire for them to have *a better future*. Whether born in the United States or resettled from another corner of the planet, whether the son of a farmworker or the daughter of a doctor, ELs enrolled in US schools represent the hope of promising opportunities for new generations.

The experience of embodying a family's dreams can be burdensome, especially when the traditions of the past collide with priorities of the present, and aspirations about the future distort current expectations. Navigating between home and school is a tough challenge for any child, but even more so for those still learning the language of instruction. Teachers may study theories and methods of teaching students from different backgrounds, but nothing can help us understand multiple facets that underlie each student's performance more than seeing the full context of the student's life. That's what stories can offer.

WHY STORIES?

The stories in this book are realistic, truthful portrayals of six English learners from preschool to community college, with details that purposefully and concisely present common attributes, issues, and situations that educators of ELs need to understand to support their success at school. Introducing you to EL students from preschool to the first year of college shows how age and grade level affect academic issues, while confirming that other factors, such as the development of oral proficiency, are surprisingly consistent for ELs regardless of age.

Written in the style of creative nonfiction, the book's stories show how various classroom and school considerations, as well as individual and family aspects, affect EL students' achievement, allowing you to dig into the story details for critical analysis. By portraying very specific issues and concerns based on real-life observations and experiences (which knowledge of second language instructional methods and theory can shed light on), the stories in this book are an efficient and compelling means of using literature to address academic topics.

College social sciences and education classes sometimes assign novels written from the perspective of a particular culture, which enable discussions about various characters, events, scenes, and other plot elements related to a course topic, such as the diaspora of a people. While this approach offers interesting insights in an engaging manner, lengthy novels include many aspects of the characters' lives that have little bearing on the content of, for example, a sociology of education course. Reading through many of those pages can feel as if you have to wade through sections to reach the more germane details for class discussion, so these short stories, whose characters, events, plots, and other elements all point toward issues that educators need to know, can be a more efficient way of using literature to teach theoretical and practical concepts. I hope the short stories in this book display immigrant family and EL experiences in a direct, yet contextualized way so that there are ample details to analyze and discuss, but few extraneous tangents. Besides, teachers will probably never know all the details of their students' lived experiences—the full novel of their lives. Short stories, as presented in this book, more closely reflect the types of details that teachers need to know the most.

The story details are a mixture of experiences that I and my students, and my colleagues and their students, have been part of and learned from. For storytelling purposes, some of the details are fictional. In general, except where permission was given to share identifying details, the names and some specifics have been changed to protect the anonymity of individuals and institutions. However, as can be with texts that blend fact and fiction, it's important to disclose that although most of this happened, all of it is True.[2]

The stories are told from a third-person perspective, similar to how a qualitative researcher describes a phenomenon they are observing while they participated in it (known as an "emic" perspective). Many times, I have written up the results of qualitative research with "rich, thick description," and in this book I push that notion further into the realm of storytelling. You, the reader, will be able to peek into the school and home life of the student and their family, as an observer who is an educator, and develop a greater understanding of the context in which the teachers, students, family, and community share lived experiences.

HOW THE BOOK IS STRUCTURED

The six chapters in this book are structured similarly, focusing on the EL's experience during a school year as well as flashbacks to the immigration story of each character's family. Keeping the time frames constant across chapters highlights the breadth of factors affecting ELs' performance at school. For example, we get a glimpse of how age of arrival in the United States may impact second language acquisition if we look at different ELs' progress over the same time period, as with many different aspects of becoming acclimated to learning in a language that is not spoken at home.

In a way, this book is an anthology of short stories about the lives of ELs at school and at home. By this, I mean that the main characters' individual stories do not intersect. However, the first three chapters take place at Settler Elementary, in Aurora, Illinois, presenting a shared setting to depict similarities and contrasts in different types of EL students and their needs. The last three chapters occur in different places, Chevron Middle School in Orlando, Florida; Alcove High School in Tyler, Texas; and Robles Community College in Los Angeles, California.

The stories' six protagonists span the ages of four to nineteen. Three of the six speak Spanish at home and the other three speak Tshiluba, Vietnamese, and Arabic, while some of them also speak indigenous, minority, or colonial languages as well.

You will meet the following ELs in chapters 1–6:

Chapter 1: Rafael, a boy in preschool, whose family is from Cuba

Chapter 2: Dibenesha, a girl in kindergarten, whose family is from the Democratic Republic of the Congo

Chapter 3: Josué, a boy in third grade, whose family is from Mexico

Chapter 4: Anh, a girl in sixth grade, whose family is from Vietnam

Chapter 5: Dani, a young man in eleventh grade, whose family is from Iraq

Chapter 6: Loredana, a young woman in the first year of college, whose family is from Venezuela

Each story begins with the student's first day at school, followed by a flashback to their family's journey to the community where the school is located. The story then recounts key events during the fall and spring semesters and ends along with the school year. After every story, an epilogue provides additional details about characters and events as well as practical and theoretical information that shed light on narrative elements. Discussion questions are also provided for individual reflection or book study groups and classes. Endnotes provide links to relevant research and resources for further consideration. My colleagues and I maintain a website, https://englishlearnerachievement.com, that includes resources for this book and links to the websites included in each chapter's endnotes, so you can access them without retyping the URLs.

As you read the stories, themes will become apparent within each and across all. I suggest that you jot down the themes you identify in the margins or at the end of a chapter so you can compare them to those highlighted in the conclusion. The conclusion discusses the book's key themes and links them, propelling you to apply what you've learned and to continue learning more.

A WORD ABOUT LANGUAGE

The stories include a number of dialogues, which are represented, for the most part, in English. As you read the dialogues, please note that when the characters are at home, with their family and community, they are written in English but understood to be spoken in the characters' native language. Dialogues at school, with classmates and teachers, are written and spoken in English, except in dual language classes or with bilingual teachers or other bilingual educators. In these cases, the dialogues either use Spanish words and sentences or signal that all or part of the dialogue is spoken in Spanish, for example, by indicating *[in Spanish]*. The English used by ELs in dialogues at school, with classmates and teachers, represents typical sentence structure of the EL student's level of English proficiency at a given moment, and it changes incrementally across time during the school year of focus for the protagonist of each story.

PRINCIPLES BEHIND THIS BODY OF WORK

English Learners at Home and at School is the fourth volume in a series of books my coauthors and I wrote that focus on English learner education, published by Harvard Education Press. All four books reflect a set of principles that motivate our work. My colleagues and I, collectively referred to as the English Learner Achievement Network (ELAN), strongly believe that:

1. Every teacher needs specific knowledge and skills for working with ELs.[3]
2. Every EL and their teacher need support from an English for Speakers of Other Languages (ESOL)/English Language Development (ELD) specialist, who has a greater depth and breadth of knowledge and skills for working with English learners.[4]
3. Every dual language or bilingual program model that serves ELs must include items 1 and 2. In other words, the English-medium instruction in every type of dual language or bilingual program model that includes ELs must be provided by teachers and other professionals with varying levels of preparation and expertise in working with EL students.

Our work began with *Preparing Every Teacher to Reach English Learners: A Practical Guide for Teacher Educators*, which lays out a model for incorporating a focus on English learners throughout university- and district-based teacher education programs.[5]

Our second book, *Educating English Learners: What Every Classroom Teacher Needs to Know*, uses case studies of four ELs to present the knowledge that teachers need to develop to meet the needs of the ELs in their classrooms.[6] This includes second language acquisition theory, second language instructional methods and curriculum, assessment for second language learners, and sociocultural aspects of second language learning and teaching.

In *Show, Tell, Build: Twenty Key Instructional Tools and Techniques for Educating English Learners*, we describe and share examples of instructional practices that are especially beneficial for ELs and show how they work for them at different English proficiency and grade levels.[7]

Our website, https://englishlearnerachievment.com, provides resources for each chapter in every book, and also offers resources for dual language teachers and programs. I encourage you to visit the website for lots of free resources and materials to help you reach your ELs.

Because informational text lends itself better to collaboration than stories, this is the only book of the series of four that has a single author. However, it represents the generous sharing of experiences, reading of drafts, and finding of obscure facts that my family, friends, colleagues, and students offered for the sole purpose of helping me write the best representation I could of the students we all know, admire, and love.

There's a reason that stories have been used to teach for millennia. Even if readers' lives are different from characters' lives, in the retelling of their experiences, we somehow feel what they are feeling. Stories, and the foundational ideas that underlie them, live within us all, no matter our origins or affiliations. With the lens of these collective, foundational ideas, we might perceive each chapter as a hero's journey or, more simply, as a fish-out-of-water tale. As my coauthors and I paraphrased communication scholars in *Educating English Learners*, the one thing of which a fish is unaware is the water. In the aquarium called the classroom, the medium we all are immersed in is *communication* (verbal and nonverbal), which both shapes and is shaped by culture. The stories of our six EL students are meant to help deepen and sharpen understanding of the role of communication and culture in ELs' academic achievement and to ignite enthusiasm for learning how to support their success.

LITERARY RESPONSES TO THE READINGS

After you read each story, here are some activities to engage with its content:[8]

1. Write a poem that expresses the character's journey and experiences.
2. Make a collage of images that tell key aspects of the story.
3. Complete a story map for the chapter.
4. Write a physical description for each of the main characters, filling in the details from your own acquaintances and experiences that they remind you of. By shading in those elements, you make the stories your own. You will notice that the EL students' physical characteristics are not described. This is simply so you can see your own students in them.
5. Write what happens during the summer or the next academic year.
6. Rewrite a scene with a different outcome and explain why that outcome was possible. If there's dialogue in the scene, rewrite it as well.
7. Write interview questions for the teachers and other educators in the story. Imagine yourself meeting with them for the interview. How would you expect them to respond? What might they say that would surprise you?
8. Each EL student's chapter is simply titled—"Rafael's Story," "Dibenesha's Story," and so on. Create a subtitle for each chapter that describes what

you think the story is about. For example, possible subtitles for *The Wizard of Oz* might be *The Journey Home* or *Journey to a Strange Land.*

EDUCATOR RESPONSES TO THE READINGS

While reading each story, *ask* the following:

What do you know *from the story* that enables you to make inferences about the EL student's performance and progress at school (academic or otherwise)? What do you know *from your own experience* that enables you to make inferences about the EL student's performance and progress at school? Consider the following suggestions to address these questions.

1. Make a three-column table for story details. In the first column, list the main details from the story; in the second, list other information about each detail that you'd like to know (e.g., the student responded well to an intervention mentioned in the story, but were other types of interventions used as well? What are the most commonly used interventions for this particular need?); and in the third column, either look up that information (if it's accessible) or suggest what it might be (see table I-1).
2. List other unmentioned story elements (e.g., what happened before a particular story event or scene, or who are other family members or friends in the student's life) that you would like to know and why (see table I-2).
3. How would any of these missing story details or elements enable you to make decisions that foster the EL student's performance and progress?
   - Note the missing story details or elements and the corresponding decisions that need to be made.
   - If you were the teacher, where could you look for the missing information?
   - What could you do if the information can't be found?
4. Have you had a similar student or experience? What did you do that was similar or different from the teacher(s) in the story?

STORY DETAIL	MORE INFORMATION ABOUT THE DETAIL THAT I'D LIKE TO KNOW	WHAT I FOUND (F) OR INVENTED (I)

TABLE I-1 Story details

UNMENTIONED STORY ELEMENTS	WHY I WANT TO KNOW

TABLE I-2 Unmentioned story elements

After reading each story, *do* the following:

Refer to the *epilogue* section at the end of the chapter for more information about selected missing story details and elements as well as a concise summary of current scholarship and resources for more in-depth study.

1. Compare your notes from questions one through four to the details provided in the epilogue.
   - What were you able to conclude correctly based on your prior knowledge?
   - What incorrect conclusions did you make based on your prior knowledge?
   - What details did you miss altogether?
   - For which issues will you consult additional resources?
2. Reflect on how you will use what you learned from this chapter and its additional resources in your own classroom.

CHAPTER 1

RAFAEL'S STORY

"Go around, go around!" the assistant principal yelled as she swept her right hand above her head like she was deflecting an invisible volleyball.

Carmen gripped the steering wheel tighter.

"You're in the bus lane! Circle around and make the *second* turn for car drop-offs!" Carmen tapped on the gas pedal lightly and steered left.

"Mami, watch out!" Rafael warned.

"Ay! I forgot to check the mirror. There are so many things to remember!"

The car inched forward, slowing the flow of incoming yellow Blue Bird school buses.

"Mami is trying her best, Rafael."

ONCE THEY MADE THE RIGHT TURN, the car pulled up to the prekindergarten drop-off, and Carmen unbuckled Rafael's booster seat. Rafael sat motionless.

"Go, Rafael, you have to go! Your teacher is there, waiting for you."

Rafael slid down and grabbed his nearly empty backpack, stepped out, and planted himself on the sidewalk, facing the building. And with that step, Carmen was alone for the first time in four years.

From when Carmen was Rafael's age, her father talked about moving to the United States. Papá was a free thinker who never hesitated to speak up, a trait that raised suspicions among leaders in the southern Cuban city of Cienfuegos. Known as "The Pearl of the South," Cienfuegos had been a major seaport since Cuba's colonial era. A key location on the old trade route between Jamaica and South America, the area was shaped by historic conflicts, including pirate invasions, Spanish American War battles, and Cuban Revolution uprisings. Once Fidel Castro gained power, Cienfuegos became a designated industrial center, as part of the revolutionary government's expansion plan. Vestiges of better times lined the avenues of Cienfuegos, with luster-less Jazz Age hotels housing schools and crumbling colonial palaces serving *cafecitos* to workers on breaks. The side streets were rutted from wear and tear caused by Chevy sedans from a bygone era, their rounded bulges chugging along on bald tires, dodging the incidental cart pulled by donkeys. Shortages have a way of forcing inventive solutions. The abundance of these jury-rigged anachronisms had come to define Cienfuegos, as did the lack of basic staples such as meat and gas.

Papá dreamed of having freedom of speech in America, fueled by his brother Anselmo who had left Cienfuegos for Chicago decades before. Uncle Anselmo had built a successful cardiology practice that allowed him to send regular remittances to his brother's family back home. Carmen's family spoke about Anselmo as if he were a distant saint bestowing blessings via Western Union. Papá planned for the eventual move of his family to the United States, but he never made it past the planning stage. Fear of the risks involved overtook his drive to leave.

After hearing all her life about Anselmo's coveted life in America, when she turned eighteen, Carmen decided to apply for the US Diversity Visa lottery. After weeks of gathering, completing, and uploading official forms and documents, she discreetly checked the State Department website and was assigned a preselection confirmation number, which she printed and kept in a lockbox hidden under her bed. Selection eluded her in that first attempt, but she wasn't discouraged, as she simply thought of the experience as practice for her successful application. Undaunted, she reapplied during the call-for-submissions period every fall.

Despite recurring rejections, Carmen never gave up on coming to the United States. After completing secondary school, she enrolled at the University of Cienfuegos to study pedagogical science, because she'd always known she wanted to work with children. While at university, she met a law student, Domingo, and fell in love, hard. Domingo and Carmen had a lot in common, from their bookishness to their family history. Both families were proud of their freedom-seeking patriarchs, who escaped from Spain to Cuba during the Spanish Civil War. Carmen and Domingo each attributed their independent streaks to their storied ancestors. Domingo loved her so deeply that he began to share her dream to emigrate, too, if that's what it would take to spend their lives together.

Right after graduation, Carmen and Domingo married in a brief civil ceremony. During their wedding dinner, the newlyweds read aloud the greeting cards from relatives who could not attend. ¡Felicidades a los novios! Tia Rosa (*Congratulations to the bride and groom! Aunt Rosa*). ¡Mis mejores deseos para los dos! Geraldo (*Best wishes to you both! Geraldo*). On and on they went, bride and groom alternating recitation, until they got to Anselmo's card, saved for last. Carmen gingerly opened the seal, but before she told the wedding guests what was written, she muttered "Ojalá," *I wish*, softly. In the envelope postmarked Chicago, IL, there were five one-hundred-dollar bills and the promise of two roundtrip tickets once Carmen and Domingo could get permission to go. More than anything, Carmen wished she and Domingo could honeymoon in the United States, but a trip there remained improbable. Nonetheless, she spoke of the gift with optimism.

"I don't know how that will ever be possible, but we will do everything we can to find a way," she proclaimed while carefully placing the envelope in her purse.

Carmen's father locked eyes with her, his eyebrows drawn in and his jaw tight. A way out never presented itself for him. As much as he wanted her wish to come true, he feared she would have to go through the same disappointment.

"Carmen, you should look into getting Spanish citizenship by descent," her cousin suggested, breaking the silence. "I know a couple people who did that. I think you both would be eligible. If you're approved, then you can apply for a US tourist visa as a Spanish citizen."

Carmen and Domingo turned toward each other inquisitively. Could that be an option?

"It can't hurt to try," Domingo affirmed.

Shortly after the wedding, they both submitted the forms and documentation for Spanish citizenship, which, serendipitously, was granted just in time for a first anniversary present. They immediately applied for a tourist visa to visit Anselmo, who, as promised, wired the money for their roundtrip tickets from Havana to Chicago, with a transfer in Cancun, once the visas were issued.

"¡Bienvenidos Carmen y Domingo! Welcome!" exclaimed Anselmo, rushing toward them as they entered the main terminal. Anselmo's wife, Silvia, sprinted to join the embrace. Behind them waited their entire Cuban American family with bilingual signs and balloons. Silvia handed Carmen a bountiful bouquet of white ginger lilies.

"Thank you, Anselmo, for making this dream vacation come true," said Domingo as he set down his carry-on bags and began to hug Carmen's extended family members, one by one. Everyone followed Carmen and Domingo to the parking garage and helped them load their suitcases into the back of Anselmo's black Suburban.

"We've all been waiting for this day," Anselmo exclaimed as he opened the back door for Carmen to climb in.

During the thirty-minute drive from the airport to Anselmo's home in Glencoe, the family talked over one another about new relationships, work promotions, degrees earned, and how much the kids had grown, here in Chicago and back in Cienfuegos.

Domingo set their suitcases on the luggage racks that Silvia had bought for the guest room and sat down in one of the two armchairs in front of the fireplace. Exhausted, Carmen joined him and kicked off her shoes.

"I'm not feeling well," she told Domingo. "Maybe I'm just tired from the trip, or it could be something I ate, but my stomach's pretty upset." Carmen picked up the folder she kept their documents in and fanned her face with it. "Do you think we can ask Anselmo to take us to a pharmacy to get an antacid?"

Domingo stood up slowly, nodded, and walked toward the living room. Anselmo was on a phone call with a patient, so he asked Silvia to drive them to the drugstore.

The florescent lights at Target made Carmen's queasiness worse. While Domingo marveled at the array of products on the shelves, Carmen wandered the store, searching for a recognizable antacid. As she walked down the aisles, the variety of pregnancy tests caught her attention. *Just in case*, she thought as she quickly grabbed the least expensive one and added it to her basket with the Alka-Seltzer. Without saying a word, she handed her two items and a $20 bill to the cashier, holding out her left hand for the change.

When Carmen got home, she took the plastic bag from Target into the bathroom. Before she took the antacid, she opened the test. It must work like the ones in Cuba, she thought, so she proceeded as she'd done before, but this time, the results were different. "Domingo, come look! Two pink lines!" she yelled joyously. "¡Que maravilloso! Maybe we should name the baby Chicago!" exclaimed Domingo.

During the next two weeks, Carmen, Domingo, and their Chicago family went shopping on the Miracle Mile, rode the elevator to the top of the Willis Tower, watched the other tourists at The Bean, and took in a boat tour along the Chicago River. As their vacation came to a close, Anselmo asked the couple to consider settling in the Chicago area. He had invested in rental properties throughout the region, and he had a two-bedroom apartment in Aurora that wasn't occupied.

Domingo started their discussion, feeling awkward about the offer. "Anselmo, that's very generous, but it's a huge step." Anselmo leaned forward and began to respond, but then Domingo talked over him. "There's a lot going on in our lives. Now isn't the time to do something so risky." Domingo's tone was definitive. There was no point in continuing.

The night before their return trip to Cuba, Carmen kept Domingo awake until dawn, discussing and debating about Anselmo's offer. Domingo took on his attorney-at-law demeanor, making a case for returning home and calmly planning a future move.

"I understand, Domingo, that rushing into a big decision can be perilous, but we don't know if we'll ever have this chance again." Carmen's lower lip trembled as she searched for the right words to convince Domingo. "If you won't do it for me, please, please do it for our baby. Our baby deserves a better future than the lives we have back home."

Later that morning when Anselmo came to help them put their bags in the SUV, Carmen and Domingo told him they had decided to stay. Awash with emotion, Anselmo ran to his home office, where he had printed the application for asylum before they even arrived, sat down with them at the breakfast table, and helped them fill it out. Carmen smiled at Domingo, and in that brief second, she thought she felt the baby move.

On the weekend, Anselmo had some free time to drive the couple over to Aurora to their two-bedroom apartment. Their place was on the first floor of a three-story concrete building with a shingled mansard roof. As Anselmo unlocked the door, Carmen and Domingo were astonished at the amount of open space, which was more pronounced because the unit was unfurnished except for a bed, two counter stools, and a loveseat. Anselmo told them that they could stay there, rent-free, for a year, which would give them time to get on their feet and find a permanent home of their own.

Carmen was bouncing with excitement.

> "Uncle Anselmo, thank you for everything you have done for us." Anselmo smiled proudly. "We love the apartment—to us it is a palace. We will do all we can to become independent as soon as possible." Carmen paused, self-consciously. "For now, though, we also need your help with something unexpected."
>
> Anselmo observed without expression, as he had learned to do in his profession.
>
> "You see, we are really glad that the apartment has two bedrooms, because . . ."

Domingo pointed to Carmen's belly, which hadn't begun to show yet.

"Do you mean a baby?!" Anselmo exclaimed. "¡Qué bendición!"

Uncle Anselmo made sure Carmen got prenatal care by using his contacts and his bank account. Slightly less than a month later, after a daily job search, Domingo got a dishwasher job at a local breakfast diner, and Carmen was hired to clean rooms at a motel franchise. Now they would have paychecks to cover groceries and utilities, and hopefully there would be some money left over to save for the baby's needs.

The day Carmen went into labor, she gave notice at the motel, and soon she settled in to being Rafael's full-time mom. To make up for Carmen's lost income, Domingo picked up extra hours and spent some of his time off watching the short-order cooks so he could move up from dishwasher pay. Carmen rarely left home, filling her days with caring for Rafael, keeping the house spotless, and cooking Cuban favorites, like her signature *ropa vieja*.

After a year in Aurora, the family relocated to a smaller apartment, which Uncle Anselmo had tried to delay until Domingo earned enough for a more suitable permanent home. Too proud to continue accepting Anselmo's generosity, Domingo picked up a second job as a busser, which expanded his time away from home to 6:00 a.m. to 9:00 p.m., six days a week. Despite their financial struggles, Carmen dedicated herself to raising Rafael, whose inquisitiveness kept her busy and whose sweetness was her reward. They loved singing, reading books, and doing crafts together.

As Rafael's first day of prekindergarten approached, Carmen started looking for work during his school hours. She applied at the motel where she previously worked, and they had an opening. Knowing that she would need to get herself to work and Rafael to prekindergarten, Carmen enrolled in driving school.

Rafael walked cautiously into his dual language classroom, taking in the colors, letters, and shapes scattered about. As he scanned the room, he saw the word *oso* next to a drawing of a furry bear.

"¡Oso!" he yelled. "Oso pardo, oso pardo, ¿Qué ves ahí?" (Brown bear, brown bear, what do you see?)

Ms. Belinda came near.

"Sí, Rafael, es un oso. Es un oso pardo. Muy bien. Bienvenido a nuestra clase, welcome to our class, Rafael!" Ms. Belinda exclaimed.

"Gracias," replied Rafael quietly.

Everywhere Rafael looked were posters, charts, and signs in English and Spanish, walls filled with words that looked very different, and some that looked alike except for an extra vowel here or a different consonant there.

"Esta es tu silla, Rafael," said Ms. Belinda as she pointed to his chair.

Rafael pulled it back from the table and sat down. One by one, the rest of the class trickled in. After the last-to-arrive preschoolers joined the circle forming on the floor, Ms. Belinda began singing the morning song.

"Buenos días, buenos días, ¿Como estas, como estas?" She clapped her hands and slapped her knees in rhythm with the melody. For the next round, the class joined in, with about half singing along, and everyone clapping and slapping. Although Rafael was shy by nature, his voice was one of the loudest, with a crescendo building up to *como estas*. Ms. Belinda grabbed her earlobes and pulled them down twice, making a clicking sound.

"Now change your ear channels to English!"

The *Frere Jacques* tune began again, but this time the lyrics were, "Good morning, good morning, how are you, how are you?"

As the students sang the first line, Ms. Belinda jerked backward with surprise. "Softly," she whispered, while moving her hand in the air as if she were pushing down a helium balloon. "We are *singing* a song, not *yelling* a song," she said with a smile. "Let's start over."

As the song began again, Rafael kept time with his hands and knees, occasionally moving his lips while he hummed the tune, all the while looking at his classmates to see if they could follow along.

Now that the tops of the cottonwood and maple trees encircling the school courtyard had transformed into shades of burgundy and amber, the self-confident chorus of preschoolers sounding out syllables extended into the hallways. Long ago Ms. Belinda stopped counting the number of teachers who asked her how she could possibly teach sounds in both languages without totally confusing the children. She used a proven method, she told them, and she stayed true to it all year long.

Knowing that Spanish has a more phonetic alphabet than English, Ms. Belinda began by teaching letter sounds *en español*. Using the principle of simple to complex, she led the class in chanting her carefully handwritten syllables whose beginning consonants resonated in the front of the mouth, *ma, me, mi, mo, mu*.

During these lessons, Ms. Belinda noticed that Rafael knew all the sounds and letters in Spanish. She began to ask him to tell the class the name of a new letter and to make its sound. Rafael hesitated at first, but with a little coaxing, he produced the right answers, which Ms. Belinda built upon to introduce key reading readiness elements to the class.

When the students were at their stations, wiggling and fidgeting on their bean bags and ball chairs, Ms. Belinda approached Rafael.

> "I really appreciate your help with teaching letters," she told him in Spanish. "How do you catch on so quickly?"
>
> Rafael crinkled his lips and nose, then broke into a smile.
>
> "My mommy helps me. She's a teacher."
>
> "I thought she was a maid," Ms. Belinda blurted without thinking.
>
> Her eyes closed, she took a deep breath, and felt it would be a long time before she could forgive herself for that comment.
>
> "She's a teacher, Ms. Belinda. She went to college to learn how to teach," Rafael asserted emphatically, then he scooched further down into the beanbag chair, turning slightly away from Ms. Belinda. "Right now she is cleaning rooms, but she is a teacher in Cuba and at our home."
>
> Ms. Belinda nodded.
>
> "Yes, she's a teacher like me, Rafael. She's an excellent teacher, and I know that because of everything she has taught you."

After the children left that day, Ms. Belinda walked into her best friend's classroom.

> "Got a minute?" she asked. "I did something really stupid." Ms. Belinda sighed, then raised her palm to her chin, kneading her fingers and thumb into her cheek. She paused before continuing with a faintly perceptible sniff, "I didn't mean to, but I feel terrible."
>
> "Oh, sweetie, we all make mistakes," said her friend, trying to think how to comfort her.
>
> Belinda told about her mouth speaking faster than her mind, and about how Rafael's mom was a certified teacher in Cuba.
>
> "Can you imagine leaving Aurora and going someplace where you don't know the language and the only job you can get is cleaning hotel rooms?" Belinda's friend inquired.

Belinda thought about this question, something she never had a reason to consider before.

"No," she said with a sigh. "Never crossed my mind until today."

The only day of the week that Domingo didn't work was Sunday, and when he *was* home, he was usually tired and cranky. Carmen's job, however, was more compatible with Rafael's schedule because she could leave the hotel once her assigned rooms were cleaned, which ordinarily was in time for school pickup. It was those late checkouts that would throw her routine awry, so she had learned to politely knock on the doors of dawdlers around 11:00.

With so much work and so little money, the family struggled mightily. Their time was tied up with work, so they couldn't take English classes, and without knowing English, their job prospects would never change. Their bare-bones income, coupled with the small window of time they could spend together, began to put a strain on everyone, Rafael included. After stressing about their money troubles, Carmen had an idea she hoped Domingo would agree with.

"Domingo, why don't we tell Uncle Anselmo that we need some help?" Domingo looked up from his recliner, his eyes slowing widening. "He's offered to lend us money many times. If we could cut back on work, we could use that time to take English classes."

Domingo glared in astonishment at Carmen for a quick moment, then he let loose. "We didn't come to America to depend on other people, Carmen!" Carmen pressed her lips tightly together and crossed her arms. "We either make an honest living here, and stand up proudly on our own feet, or we might as well go back to Cuba." Domingo nodded, as if he was agreeing with himself. Carmen stared back, completely still.

The thought of returning to Cienfuegos unnerved Carmen because she feared that this time Domingo's threat wasn't a bluff. His mother, who was a widow, had not been well, and she had pleaded with him increasingly to come home to care for her. Domingo had long been discouraged that he couldn't practice law, and despite his hard work and ambition, he had only moved up to a busser position. Their persistent problems were forming a perfect storm, and Domingo was threatening to evacuate.

Carmen thought their talk was over when Domingo stood up, but he pressed on.

"What if I go back to Cuba to help my mom for a couple months, and then we can decide if we all should move back?" Domingo proposed dispassionately.

Carmen reeled back, the left side of her upper lip curling upward. This was too much.

"Are you crazy, Domingo?! Have you lost your mind?!" She tapped her forehead twice and scoffed. "You know there won't be a warm welcome for you or anyone who has left the country. And even if we could get past the stigma of returning from the US, if we changed our mind, there is no chance of leaving Cuba again." Domingo stood up straighter and faced Carmen head on. Unfazed, she continued. "You are talking about throwing away everything we have fought and worked for just because we haven't accomplished our dream yet—that's ridiculous!"

"What's going on?" Rafael asked as he walked into the living room, barefoot, in his pajamas.

"Nothing! Nothing. Go back to bed," Domingo scolded.

"OK," Rafael responded. "The noise scared me. Will you read me a story?"

Carmen nodded and followed Rafael, grabbing his latest favorite book, *Siempre te querré*, from the shelf.

Although he had been very shy at the beginning of the school year, little by little Rafael came out of his shell. He was raising his hand to answer questions in Spanish within a couple weeks of starting preschool, and by March, he actually began raising his hand to answer in English.

Lately, however, he had become more withdrawn, regressing to his earlier shyness. Ms. Belinda kept an eye on his behavior for few days before she decided to check in with him.

"Rafael, you haven't been answering questions in class. Are you feeling well? Is everything OK?"

Rafael rolled a thick magic marker back and forth on the table.

"Rafael?" Ms. Belinda said with an exaggerated rising intonation.

"I don't know," he whispered.

"You can tell me, Rafael," Ms. Belinda said.

Rafael sat silently.

"Is someone or something upsetting you?" Ms. Belinda kept on.

"I got in trouble . . ." Rafael trailed off.

"Who said you are in trouble?"

"Papi," Rafael said almost inaudibly.

"Honey, what happened with Papi?"

Rafael looked down at his shoes.

"My mami is mad at my papi, and my papi is mad at me."

Ms. Belinda placed her hand on Rafael's forearm.

"How do you know they are angry?"

Rafael picked at his jacket zipper.

"Mami yells at Papi, and Papi yells at me."

That evening, after hesitating to use her high-intermediate-level classroom Spanish skills in an adult conversation, Ms. Belinda called Carmen, who explained their family's financial situation and dreams deferred. Carmen told Ms. Belinda how much it meant to her to be able to speak with her in Spanish, and she unburdened her deepest concerns on that call.

The next day, every time Ms. Belinda looked at Rafael, there was a two-second delay, a nearly imperceptible lingering caused by having stepped into his world outside of school. So much to consider, so much explained.

This year the children responded amazingly well to Ms. Belinda's reading readiness program, and by May they were decoding syllables at kindergarten level in Spanish and English. In fact, this year's assessments were the best of the three years that Ms. Belinda taught at Settler Elementary's prekindergarten.

By the end of preschool, Rafael could comfortably converse in two languages, and who knew how many bilingual songs he could sing! He was in the upper quartile of his class's reading readiness assessment in English, and he adored school. He couldn't wait to start kindergarten.

"Hola, Mami," Rafael called out to Carmen in the school cafeteria.

"Hola, Rafael!"

Ms. Belinda came near.

"Sra. Pérez, it's so nice to see you here!"

Carmen smiled, nodded, and turned to get back to the kitchen.

"Rafael, everyone loves Sra. Pérez. She is so wonderful with all the children."

"I know," said Rafael, "she is a great teacher and a great cook!"

After Settler Elementary had hired Carmen for a vacant cafeteria worker position, Ms. Belinda worked out childcare arrangements for her to enroll in Settler's community adult ESL class that started right after work.

"You know, Mrs. Pérez," said Ms. Belinda, "we always need bilingual teachers' aides. I think you could work your way toward a position once you finish all the English levels."

Carmen let out a nervous laugh. "Ojalá, that would be a dream come true," she replied.

With her new job's better pay and benefits, along with the school's summer bridge program that both mother and son were part of, Carmen's increased income allowed Domingo to quit his bussing job and attend night school ESL classes. In recognition of his strong work ethic and ambition to advance, the diner promoted Domingo to short-order cook. They were finally on their way.

Once they got their finances in order, Domingo and Carmen decided to cash one of their paychecks each month and send it to Domingo's mother so she could get more care at home, and the first amount they wired included a little extra so she could purchase a smartphone to video chat with them once a week. It was now Domingo's and Carmen's turn, and privilege, to send their first remittance to family in Cuba.

EPILOGUE

Birth Home (or Family's Place of Origin) to US Home

A tropical island whose land mass is similar in size to Tennessee, Cuba is south of the United States and north of Jamaica. To its southeast is Haiti and the Dominican Republic and to its west is the Yucatan Peninsula of Mexico. Cuba is bounded by the Caribbean Sea on its south coast and the North Atlantic Ocean on its north coast. The largest country in the Caribbean, Cuba is mainly flat, with rugged mountains in the southeast. About 80 percent of Cuba's population of 11 million live in urban areas, and its literacy rate is 99.8 percent.[1]

Cuba is a communist state that maintains strong political control, but its economic system is adopting policies that permit ownership of property and some private enterprise. Due to a trade embargo, the United States does not import Cuban-made products.[2] A survey of Cuban household incomes indicated that approximately 50 percent of Cubans have a median household income of $300 to $400 per year, but their health care and education are free, and their housing is heavily subsidized. In addition, a growing number of Cubans add to their state employment incomes through tips or sales earned in self-employed side jobs in tourist areas.[3]

Community in the United States

In 2017, Cuba and the United States agreed to allow Cubans who set foot on US land to stay, but if apprehended at sea, they have to be sent back to Cuba. This is part of a history of Cuban migration to the United States after the establishment of Cuba's communist government. The Cuban diaspora encompassed Spain, Puerto Rico, and other Latin American and Caribbean countries as well as the US, which is home to the largest number of Cuban expatriates.

Cuban migration to the US occurred in phases affected by political events in Cuba and the US. The first wave of Cuban migrants, approximately 250,000 individuals, arrived after the Cuban Revolution in 1959, which was the beginning of the greatest influx of refugees in US history. Following this initial period of exodus from 1959 to 1962, the Freedom Flights, or *Los Vuelos de la Libertad*, brought another 250,000 emigrants to Miami, Florida, from 1965 to 1973. In 1980, the harbor in Mariel, Cuba, was opened for flotillas of exiles to depart, with a total of approximately 125,000 reaching Key West, Florida. Another 30,000 Cubans left in 1994 when restrictions on migration between both countries changed. After the fall of the Soviet Union, another period of migration occurred from 1995 to 2017, with 650,000 emigrants leaving Cuba for the US.[4]

Recent estimates indicate that 2.3 million individuals of Cuban origin reside in the US. Cuban Americans are far more likely to be foreign born than other Latinx residents of the US, with 56 percent of Cubans born outside of the US versus 33 percent of all Hispanic Americans. Cuban Americans have higher levels of educational attainment than Hispanics in general. Twenty-five percent of Cuban Americans over the age of twenty-five have bachelor's degrees versus 16 percent of US Hispanics. Cuban Americans' poverty levels are slightly lower than other Hispanics (14 percent versus 17 percent, respectively).[5]

According to the Pew Research Center, there are more than 60 million Hispanics in the US, the second-fastest-growing ethnic/racial group (Asian Americans are the fastest-growing group). The main places of origin of Hispanic Americans are Mexico (62 percent), followed by Puerto Rico (10 percent), with Cuba and El Salvador both at 4 percent. Hispanic Americans from Venezuela, the Dominican Republic, Guatemala, and Honduras have experienced the greatest population increase in the last decade. Overall, Latino immigrants are a declining portion of the US Latino population, and 37 percent of Hispanic immigrants speak English proficiently.

Rafael is from Cuba, considered a Caribbean country. Latin Americans from Caribbean regions include Puerto Ricans and Dominicans. In addition, the Caribbean region is the home of non-Hispanic immigrant groups in the US, such as Haitian Americans. In *Educating English Learners*, my coauthors and I present stories of a Haitian kindergartner, Gero, and a Puerto Rican tenth grader, Edgar, along with discussions of their places and cultures of origin.

School

Rafael is fortunate that Settler Elementary has a free, high-quality prekindergarten program, and even more fortunate that it provides a dual language immersion program. English learners from birth to third grade who are acquiring English in addition to their home language are also called dual language learners because using two language systems during this early developmental period offers unique affordances. During early childhood development, the process of first language acquisition is actively ongoing, and the second language acquisition process both mirrors and complements it. Although there is a widespread assumption that children learn second languages effortlessly and quickly, the outcome can vary due to individual, contextual, and instructional factors. This means that learning English as a second language can happen successfully and promptly for young children when optimal learning environments and support are provided.

Early childhood education programs have been shown to have substantial benefits for students throughout their school years. According to the Learning Policy Institute, attending preschool better prepares students for school, and every dollar invested in preschool returns $17 in educational expenditures over time.[6] In a review of over fifty years of studies, researchers found that attending preschool reduces identification for special education and grade retention by eight percentage points and increases high school graduation by twelve percentage points.[7]

Dual language education uses English and a partner language to learn language/literacy and academic subjects, and it aims for all children to reach bilingual, biliterate, and bicultural competence in both languages. More specifically, the type of dual language education program that Rafael is enrolled in is known as two-way dual language immersion because his class is composed of children whose families speak English at home as well as children whose families speak Spanish at home, ideally represented in equal proportions. In other words, because instruction is in both languages and builds on the home languages of the children, which, in turn, enables them to become proficient in their second languages, half of Rafael's class is English learners and the other half is Spanish learners.

When all students participate in the process of becoming bilingual, a greater appreciation of the process and product of second language acquisition can result. This is in contrast with programs that use only English with EL students, and that might, unintentionally, foster the impression that they come to school with a deficit in language and literacy rather than having the asset of oral proficiency (and possibly literacy) in another language. When the children from English-speaking homes are also learning a new language of instruction, there is a greater chance that they will better understand their English learner peers' successes and challenges in learning a new language. Dual language programs in the United States are offered in a variety of languages, with Spanish being by far the most prevalent. Many conditions need to be in place to consider establishing a dual language program, such as an adequate number of speakers of the partner language in the area, the availability of qualified teachers, and a community that supports the approach.

Research indicates that English learners can reach higher levels of achievement in dual language classrooms than in other program models.[8] Specific cognitive benefits of learning in two languages include increased ability to direct attention successfully, or what is termed executive function, as well as higher levels of language awareness. There are affective benefits as well, such as greater empathy and appreciation of cultural differences.[9]

Dual language immersion is especially valuable at the prekindergarten age because instruction focuses on naming and labeling concrete objects, and doing so in two languages provides equal advantages for using oral proficiency that children have developed in their home language to become literate in both languages. As my coauthors and I have illustrated in *Educating English Learners*, language demands rise and non-linguistic representations, such as graphics, descend as students progress through the grade levels.[10]

Because students typically develop pre-reading skills in prekindergarten, dual language immersion programs teach letters and their sounds in both languages, which takes advantage of the commonalities between languages. In the case of Spanish and English, their shared alphabetic writing system enables children to build a common foundation for reading.

Many dual language preschool programs begin by teaching sounds and symbols in Spanish, which has a very regular and intuitive spelling system, or *predictable orthography*, that fosters decoding. Ms. Belinda's *ma, me, mi, mo, mu* activity exemplifies that approach, which typically starts by teaching Spanish's five vowel sounds and symbols (English has twelve vowel sounds and five symbols, a more complex association than Spanish's one to one) and then blends them into syllables by fronting them with a consonant. Because the Spanish orthography is much more logical than that of English, students may accurately decode Spanish texts beyond their ability to comprehend them. It is important to avoid conflating reading accuracy and comprehension for students learning to read in Spanish, especially because these elements are more closely connected when learning to read in English.[11]

Rafael was also fortunate that Ms. Belinda was his teacher. Although Ms. Belinda is proficient in Spanish, English is her dominant language, and she works hard to ensure that both languages have equal prominence and value in her classroom. When she heard students' rendition of the "Good Morning" song with more volume than the "Buenos Días" one, she guided the children to sing both with equal enthusiasm.

Family

Many immigrant families experience financial struggles just as Rafael's parents did. Having relatives in the United States is a definite advantage for a host of reasons, but sometimes financial support is beyond the wherewithal of relatives who are established in the US. In other cases, as with Domingo, pride can prevent families from asking for or accepting help.

The stress of immigrating, which includes becoming accustomed to new ways of doing things and different cultural norms, as well as learning a new language, are compounded by financial concerns. Immigrant families can feel trapped by the need to earn enough to make ends meet.

Depending on the region from which immigrants depart, and the reason they did so, there are wide ranges in levels of education and professional preparation. It's not unusual for immigrants to have earned degrees from their home countries that they cannot use in the United States, at least until they become proficient in English.

Virtually every person who moves to the United States not knowing the main language understands that English is the most valuable commodity they can obtain. But because their previous experiences and education matter little if they don't speak English, many immigrants work nonskilled, low-paying jobs that won't cover basic living expenses, so they add on a second or even a third one, leaving no time for English study. And if you ask them if they aspire to the American Dream, they'll often tell you that they dream for their children, not themselves. Ms. Belinda intervened on Carmen's behalf and set her up for advancement over time as a school employee.

Student

Rafael is an only child who is intimidated by new sights, sounds, and events. He seeks the familiar and is comfortable only after a new experience turned out positive. Ms. Belinda saw his reluctance to join in, and she made small and frequent overtures to convince Rafael that he was safe. In getting to know him over time, she immediately noticed when he was distressed. Approaching him with open-ended questions, she learned about his parents' conflicts at home and spoke with a counselor in case a referral would be necessary. Ultimately, she offered support that impacted their problems at home.

RAFAEL'S STORY DISCUSSION QUESTIONS

1. Carmen handed a $20 bill to the cashier at Target and hoped for the best because she hadn't used the currency system in the US yet. Have you ever felt completely lost and confused in another country? What was that experience like? How do you think Carmen felt?
2. The children in Ms. Belinda's class sang the English version of the song louder than the Spanish version. Why do you think they did that? How do children come to know that one language is perceived as more important than another?
3. Ms. Belinda regretted her comments to Rafael about Carmen's profession. Have you ever blurted something out to a student without thinking? How did you make it right? How did you learn from it?
4. Rafael's parents' dream was to live freely and to be able to work hard and earn a decent living so that Rafael could have better opportunities than they had. How is Rafael's family's dream different from the dreams of families born in the US? How is it similar?
5. Ms. Belinda called Carmen to discuss Rafael's withdrawal from classroom interactions, which she found out from him was caused in part by issues at home. Have you ever contacted a parent about something a child told you about their home life? What was that experience like? If you haven't, would you be willing to? Why or why not?
6. Rafael and his family depended on their family members who had moved to the US before their immigration to the Chicago area. What would Rafael's family's experience have been like if they hadn't had family in the US?

7. Carmen's father raised her with a desire for freedom of speech and a penchant for independent thinking, which led her to dream of moving to the US. Do you think seeking freedom from government control over most aspects of life is a more important or honorable reason for immigrating to the US than other reasons? Why or why not?

CHAPTER 2

DIBENESHA'S STORY

"Wake up, Dibenesha! Hurry, get up now!"

Benga shook her daughter's shoulder as the little girl opened her eyes.

"You can't be late for your first day of school! Being on time is *very* important in America!"

They had been waiting for this day for months—years, actually. Benga's alarm rang at 6:00 a.m., but she slept right through it, eventually waking from the sounds of nearby road construction that started at 7:30.

"The bus will be here in fifteen minutes. Go brush your teeth!"

THE BUS TO SETTLER ELEMENTARY took thirty minutes, but it was a world away from Dibenesha's life so far. Dibenesha was born in the Democratic Republic of the Congo, near the Angolan border. She was raised by her parents, Benga and Majumbu, along the banks of the Kasai, a tributary of the massive Congo River. When she was barely three, Dibenesha was awakened by her mother's screaming. Dibenesha trembled as Benga lunged toward her, blocking her view of Majumbu's body. They clung to each other, motionless, as a militia of five ransacked their home, checking for anyone else on their hit list who might be hiding. As the last of the five men left the house, he turned and lit a cotton rag that was stuffed into a gas-filled bottle and hurled it through the front door. Benga and Dibenesha ran through the blaze and into the basin forest, careful to keep undetected until the light of day.

The next year of Dibenesha's life unfolded in an Angolan refugee camp, where she and her mother waited for permission to emigrate to a host country. Each day passed slowly in the crowded compound, and the nights' impenetrable darkness was interrupted by a mere thirty minutes of electricity, powered by a four-inch solar panel that a relief organization donated to every family. Benga's and Dibenesha's days were structured around mealtimes, with copious amounts of downtime in between.

Dibenesha was too small to help gather water or prepare food rations, so she occupied herself by drawing or playing with a small car fashioned from discarded jars and bottle tops that a little boy gave her when he and his family were granted asylum by Sweden. Whenever Dibenesha found a lid or a wire, she would replace worn-out or less functional parts of the car, and it soon began to look and go like a real toy. She attached a tattered jute string to the front to pull the car along, and she used a broken brick to prop up a scrap of tin at a thirty-degree angle, launching the car from the top. The toy car provided hours of daily recreation, and improving it was a source of endless fascination. Benga praised each new enhancement that Dibenesha showed her.

At the time of their intake to the refugee camp, Benga had told the official that her first choice for asylum was "the United States of America, the land of opportunity." Throughout Benga's life, she had heard about America's promise, and she wanted a chance for Dibenesha to experience it. On an ordinary, sweltering day, just over one year from when they arrived at the camp, Benga and Dibenesha were called to meet with an official who was clearly bearing good news. They were going to America.

There wasn't much to pack, but Benga and Dibenesha each had one essential item tucked into their bag. Benga had carefully wrapped the solar panel in newspaper because, she told Dibenesha, "we might need power in America." Dibenesha looked around at the children at play, teetering an old bicycle tire along with a stick, hesitated for a moment, and placed her little car on top of her clothes. "We might need toys in America," she told her mother, authoritatively.

After one bus ride and two flights, one of which was very, very long, Benga and Dibenesha arrived at Chicago O'Hare Airport. Waiting at the airport was a representative from a resettlement agency, HIAS, to take them to their apartment in Aurora, about an hour's drive, due west, from the terminal.

"Benga?" asked the case worker when he saw the two exiting the tram. "Welcome to Chicago! I'm Kaleb, originally from Ethiopia, and now, Illinois," he exclaimed as he swept his extended arm across the expanse of the airport lobby.

"I like it here," Kaleb continued, "but you have to get used to winter—it's *so* cold. Tomorrow I'll take you to the office. We have a storage room full of warm clothes, and you can keep any you like that fit. It's still summer here, but you'll need them sooner than you think."

It wasn't long, indeed, until Benga and Dibenesha were bundled in goose down, for the summer evenings struck them with a wind colder than any they'd experienced before. Together they walked in their puffer coats, past their neighbors sitting outside in short sleeves. The clothes weren't the only help they received from the resettlement agency. During their first year in the United

States, they were given a small monthly stipend to partially subsidize their expenses, and Kaleb introduced them to two Congolese families who called the same area of northeastern Illinois home. Within a week of arrival, Benga began taking adult English as a Second Language (ESL) classes for beginners at a nearby community school, and her new friends from back home babysat Dibenesha. It only took Benga a month to land a part-time job, helping to care for the elderly in a small, privately owned retirement home, and she was proud to be able to set aside a portion of her salary to compensate her friends for childcare.

Toward the end of their first year in the US, Benga began preparing Dibenesha for kindergarten. "Soon you will be going to school," said Benga eagerly. "You are going to learn so much. I'm going to walk with you every morning to the school bus, and when the school day is over, I will be waiting for your bus, exactly where I kissed you goodbye in the morning."

Dibenesha listened attentively. Some of Dibenesha's Congolese friends had told her about bus rides and backpacks and center time, and it all sounded wonderful and exciting.

Dibenesha did make it onto the bus on the first day of school, after all that worry and hurry caused by Benga's oversleeping. The school was actually farther from her home than she had traveled during the entire past year, and the new sights held her attention for the half-hour commute. Unsure of what was expected of her, Dibenesha watched her future classmates closely, imitating and following their actions. Once she got to the kindergarten classroom, Dibenesha saw Mr. Davies, her teacher, standing in the doorway. She wanted to tell him that she had been waiting for this day, and that she was ready to learn everything they teach in kindergarten, but her words didn't belong to his language, and all she could do was look up with a shy smile as he spoke in streams of consonants and vowels, some sounding familiar, some not. Realizing quickly that Dibenesha was a newcomer, Mr. Davies, like a silent movie actor, suddenly didn't need dialogue; he used his face, even his whole body, to show his extraordinary depth of caring. Although Mr. Davies didn't understand Dibenesha's language, somehow she felt heard.

The bright-colored array of alphabet charts, blocks, and art supplies drew Dibenesha further into the room. Following the actions of the other kindergartners, she hung her backpack on her designated hook, walked over to the large, rectangular alphabet rug centered in front of the teacher's easel chart and rocking chair, and sat on the letter Y. Soon most letters had a wiggly occupant, and Mr. Davies walked up to the easel, calling everyone to attention.

"Criss-cross applesauce!" he said as every knee bent in response.

The children sitting on letters X and Z pointed to Dibenesha's ankles.

"What's that? What happened to your skin?"

Dibenesha tucked her legs in tighter and covered her ankles with her hands.

Mr. Davies heard the commotion in the back. "One, two, three, eyes on me," he called out.

After introducing himself to the class, he asked each student to say their name. When they got to the next-to-last student, she said *dee-ben-eh'-shah* before Mr. Davies could call on her. Mr. Davies smiled and took over, restating her name and telling the class that she speaks another language, Tshiluba, and that she is learning English.

"We are so lucky to have Dibenesha in our class," said Mr. Davies. "She can help us learn about where she is from. It will take her a while to start speaking English, so we need to be kind and helpful as she gets used to being in school in America."

Dibenesha's eyes darted left and right as the other carpet sitters turned toward her, and she let out a sigh as Mr. Davies moved on to Z.

After the school day ended, Mr. Davies poked his head in the doorway of the classroom next to his.

"Hey, how'd it go?"

"Better than expected," said the teacher, who was starting her last year before retirement.

"Good! My day was pretty smooth, but there was a moment when some of the kiddos began pointing to the burn scars of a student who doesn't speak English. I got the class back on track, but I wish I could have reassured her better. She looked petrified."

"Oh wow, I heard about a refugee family that set their apartment on fire the night they moved in." The teacher starting laughing, then rolled her eyes and shook her head. "Yeah, apparently they tried to make dinner how they used to back home, so they lit a fire in the living room, and it spread across the carpet. My brother's one of the firefighters that responded, and he couldn't believe what set the fire off. I bet that's how she got burned."

Mr. Davies shook his head slightly, not wanting to encourage speculation.

"We don't know if it was her family. There are other refugee families in this area, so it's hard to tell."

"Well, whether it was her family or not, I think you're going to have a hard time getting her accustomed to school."

"Maybe so, but I have a feeling she's going to be OK," said Mr. Davies as he turned to head back to his room.

In the time that passed since that first day, Dibenesha's personality began to emerge. Mr. Davies took note of her engagement and participation, which showed an incremental, steady increase. She was getting accustomed to school, to the classroom, to her classmates, and to him. The school's new ELD resource teacher, Ms. Regent, had started to check in with Mr. Davies, and her suggestions were very helpful. Because Mr. Davies always seemed appreciative, Ms. Regent felt comfortable offering suggestions of how he might do something better. In one case, Mr. Davies was going over eight words in a "Read it, Write it, Highlight it" handout with the class, focusing on identifying the simple, phonetic spellings, such as *pin* and *bin*, in short sentences. The instant that Mr. Davies called on the class for each answer, Dibenesha was the first to raise her hand. Surprised by her readiness, Mr. Davies told her to go to the interactive whiteboard and point to the word, and to his relief, she was absolutely right.

Watching from the back of the room, Ms. Regent nodded to Mr. Davies, whose smile back also signaled to Dibenesha that the first risk she took in class had paid off. Once the students went to their centers, the ELD teacher gestured to Mr. Davies to follow her. Together they walked to Dibenesha's table.

"Dibenesha, you are learning to read very well," said Ms. Regent. You know your letters and their sounds. You found the word *pin* in the sentence right away!"

Dibenesha beamed.

"Do *you* have any pins, Dibenesha?"

Dibenesha smiled.

After a few seconds, Mr. Davies repeated the question. Dibenesha's gaze fell to her desk.

"Don't be shy, Dibenesha. Can you tell us if you have any pins?"

Dibenesha's expression tightened.

Ms. Regent took over, pointing to the MATH pin on her shirt lapel.

"Dibenesha, this is a pin."

She unlocked the clasp and took the pin off, careful to reclose it before handing it to Dibenesha.

"We call it a pin because we pin it to something, usually our clothes."

With that, Ms. Regent extended her palm, retrieved the pin, and pushed the prong through her collar's fabric, fastening it securely.

"I just *pinned* my *pin* to my shirt."

Dibenesha laughed quietly and looked up.

"Pin," she said confidently.

"That's right Dibenesha, *pin*," confirmed Mr. Davies.

Mr. Davies thought about how quickly Dibenesha was learning to spell and to recognize words, but with Ms. Regent's help, he saw how Dibenesha needed something more than students who were raised speaking English. The class had finished the "Read it" and "Highlight it" sections of the handout, and he planned to assign completing the "Write it" section for homework. But now he knew that he needed to enhance the assignment. During his planning period, he added clip art next to the eight words and printed the revised version.

Dibenesha carefully placed the handout in her backpack, put on her jacket, and then her puffer coat, knit cap, and wool mittens before she left for the bus. By the time the bus got to her stop, the sun was slowly descending toward the horizon. There stood Benga, her face covered with a scarf to block the December wind.

"I'm making your favorite dinner. Let's hurry home so we can finish cooking and eat!"

Once home, Dibenesha watched intently as Benga added spices to the simmering pot.

"Another five minutes!" Benga exclaimed.

About a minute later, the burner stopped working. Benga turned it off and back on again. Nothing. She tried the other burners. None worked. She flipped the light switch. No electricity.

"Mama, what happened?"

Benga told a little fib. "I don't know."

"Will it come back on, Mama?"

Benga had been worried about the electricity for the ten days that had passed since last month's bill was due. Kaleb at HIAS had told her about making sure to pay bills on time, but because the retirement home had cut her hours the month before, her paycheck didn't cover her expenses. The electric bill was the smallest, so she chose to pay it late.

Soon the winter sky withdrew the natural light from the apartment, and Dibenesha began to sob.

"Don't be afraid of the dark. It's OK," Benga said as she pulled Dibenesha to her side.

"No, Mama, that's not it! I, I have homework. Mr. Davies will be waiting for it tomorrow, but I can't do it in the dark!"

Benga headed toward her bedroom, which, facing south, was the warmest and brightest spot in their home.

"Come, come," she said.

Dibenesha grabbed her backpack and followed.

Benga reached behind the curtain and picked something up from the corner of the windowsill.

"I told you that someday we might need power," Benga said as she connected the nightstand lamp to the four-inch solar panel.

Dibenesha jumped onto the bed with her backpack, pencil in hand.

After returning from winter break, the whole school was treated to a local production of *Beauty and the Beast*. Dibenesha sang along with the girls sitting by her, well prepared after watching the DVD many times with her friends. Once back in the classroom, Mr. Davies wrote something on the whiteboard to start their discussion of the play.

"Bonjour!" said Dibenesha in perfectly accented French, before Mr. Davies could pronounce the written words for the class.

Everyone stared at Dibenesha, who continued, *"Je m'appelle Dibenesha, et je parle français. Les gens de la République Démocratique du Congo parlent français."*

Dibenesha's records indicated that she spoke Tshiluba, a language prevalent in the Kasai area, but there was no mention of French. Throughout the discussion, Mr. Davies referred to Dibenesha to pronounce French words, which she eagerly did with great panache.

The spring semester seemed to fly by, and Mr. Davies watched Dibenesha's progress with wonder. Here was a girl from the other side of the world, who came to his class knowing no English, and who now is able to speak three languages. In fact, Dibenesha learned English faster than any student he taught, ever. It all would have been perfect except for one issue. Once a week or so, Dibenesha was coming to school late. During the fall, it happened a couple of times, but now she arrived late more often. Around the end of September, Mr. Davies reached out to Benga, arranging a phone call with an interpreter service, but he wasn't able to get in contact with her. Now that Dibenesha was able to understand conversations in English, Mr. Davies decided to bring it up.

"Dibenesha, I've noticed that you are coming to school late. What's going on?"

Dibenesha smiled faintly.

"It's OK. You're not in trouble. I just want to understand why."

Mr. Davies stayed silent, waiting for a response.

Dibenesha tugged at her hair.

"It's really OK . . . You can tell Mr. Davies. Is there a reason you're coming late?"

"My mom, she can't sleep. She hears sounds. Sometimes she sees flashing lights through her window. She can only sleep when it's not dark outside."

Mr. Davies nodded slowly as Dibenesha explained. "I'm going to see if I can help."

Near the front lobby, the school stored student records in the Cume Room, so named to quickly refer to what was officially known as the Student Cumulative Records Office. Mr. Davies had received initial paperwork for Dibenesha when school started, but he thought he'd check the Cume to see if anything had been added. On top of the papers in the folder was an intake sheet from HIAS, listing contact information for Dibenesha's caseworker, Kaleb. Mr. Davies sat down and dialed the number.

"HIAS, this is Kaleb," a friendly voice announced.

"Hi, Kaleb. This is Mr. Davies, a kindergarten teacher at Settler Elementary. My student, Dibenesha, had your contact information in her Cume file. Do you have a minute?"

"Sure. Yes. How can I help?"

Mr. Davies looked down at the Cume and asked, "I haven't been able to speak with Dibenesha's mother. Could you help me get in touch with her?"

"Oh, no. I'm sorry to hear that," Kaleb replied. "I apologize for not being in touch sooner, but I'm just returning from emergency medical leave."

"That's OK. Glad you're doing better," Mr. Davies interjected.

"An intern filled in for me while I was out, but I'm finding that some things, like getting Dibenesha's paperwork to Settler, fell through the cracks. Mr. Davies, let me tell you a few things about Dibenesha and her mother before I put you in touch."

Kaleb recounted the whole story, from the small home in the Democratic Republic of the Congo that Dibenesha shared with Benga and Majumbu, to the night of the assassination and its terrible effects. The burns on Dibenesha's legs, Benga's fear of home invasions during the night. All of it. He described life in the refugee camp, explaining why Dibenesha always kept her backpack in sight, because for a long time, all she had was what she carried. Mr. Davies pulled the phone away from his face, struggling for composure before responding.

The next day Mr. Davies felt like he knew Dibenesha in a different way. Most notably, it was established, now and forevermore, that his admiration of her character and accomplishments was unlimited, just as he perceived her potential.

When he spoke with Benga, Mr. Davies had already arranged to have a donated alarm system installed at their apartment, something she was unfamiliar with at the time but grew to depend on for sound sleep. Soon, Dibenesha arrived on time every day.

Now that the school year was winding down, the kindergarten classes were planning a big "makers" activity as part of their Schoolwide Enrichment Model (SEM), so to start off the unit, Mr. Davies asked everyone to bring something from home that they made, either by themselves or with their family or caregivers. All kinds of items were pulled out of backpacks, from Kleenex box holders to bird feeders. When it was Dibenesha's turn, she walked to the front of the alphabet carpet and proudly held up the little car made of bottle tops, empty jars, PVC scraps, and discarded wires. The kindergartners stared silently, their faces crinkled with skepticism. Dibenesha wrapped the jute pull string into a wad and stuffed it into the center of the car. She took a piece of cardboard and two books and fashioned a makeshift ramp.

"See how fast my car goes!" Dibenesha exclaimed, as she loosened her grasp of the car perched on top of the ramp.

It stopped a few inches past the end, so she added two more books underneath the cardboard, and did it again. This time the car stopped a foot away.

"See how far my car goes!"

Half of the class had already "uncrossed their applesauce" and were up and ready to rush the table. "It's so cool, right?!" Mr. Davis said. "I know everyone wants to try it, but we'll have to take turns."

Ms. Donato, the gifted program coordinator who had organized the SEM activity, had been standing just inside the doorway since the first student had showed their project and told about it. When the class went to lunch, she asked to speak to Mr. Davies.

"I really enjoyed your maker lesson launch," Ms. Donato acclaimed. The children brought so many creative projects. The one that stood out most, I think, was the car made from recycled parts. I see evidence of high achievement capability."

Mr. Davies let the last sentence sink in. *High achievement capability* described the little girl who learned conversational English rapidly, who had developed above grade-level literacy skills in English and French, and who perfected a car and ramp, made of trash, that took advantage of the laws of physics.

Ms. Donato suggested that Mr. Davies start a log of his observations, interactions, and classroom assessments of Dibenesha to track her learning progress, beginning the process of identification for giftedness. Mr. Davies reached out to Ms. Regent, the ELD teacher, to join this process as well. With a nonverbal ability assessment scheduled for the last week of May, Dibenesha was on her way toward gifted programming upon entering first grade the next year. She was the first refugee Mr. Davies had taught, and even though some teachers with more experience had doubts about Dibenesha's capability, fortunately Mr. Davies never did.

EPILOGUE

Birth Home (or Family's Place of Origin) to US Home

Dibenesha was born in the Democratic Republic of the Congo, also known as DRC, which gained independence from Belgium in 1960. A country whose population tops 100 million, DRC's land mass comprises about a fourth of the US mainland. There is variation in typical weather between the land north and south of the equator, as well as between the low-lying and mountainous areas, but the country's proximity to the equator makes its climate tropical. There are over two hundred ethnic groups, with the majority belonging to the Bantu language family. Although French is the official language, four regional languages are also spoken by DRC's population. Approximately 77 percent of the population is literate.[1]

A protracted civil war ended in 2003; however, there has been persistent political unrest in the country, which has resulted in the United Nations Peacekeeping operation's presence in DRC since 2010. Since 2016 the Kasai region has been the center of violent conflict driven by militias with allegiance to opposing forces, with hundreds of thousands of residents in this area escaping to Angola, Zambia, and other countries that border DRC. Many of these refugees have no idea why their families were targets of violence.[2]

The UN Refugee Agency's definition of a refugee is "someone who has been forced to flee his or her country because of persecution, war, or violence." [3] Benga and Dibenesha were refugees that lived temporarily in a facility commonly referred to as a refugee camp. The UN-supported refugee camp in neighboring Angola provided them with medical care, food, shelter, and essential supplies and determined that they qualified for refugee status. Because refugees are from different countries and continents, their experiences can differ greatly. In fact, only 40 percent of refugees flee to camps, the largest of which are primarily in Africa. Many refugees from other parts of the world relocate to urban areas, with Turkey accommodating the biggest population. Once Benga and Dibenesha received refugee status from the UN Refugee Agency, they were referred to the US Refugee Admissions Program for consideration.[4] After approval, they had medical exams, participated in a cultural orientation, and received a loan to travel to the United States. The US State Department Bureau for Population, Refugees, and Migration worked with HIAS to select Aurora, Illinois, as their new residence.

Community in the United States

Once in the US refugees are generally provided with about eight months of funding for basic needs and medical care, coordinated by the Office of Refugee Resettlement, a division of the US Department of Health and Human Services.[5] In partnership with a total of nine nonprofit organizations, the Office of Refugee Resettlement also assists families by enrolling them in ESL and job training classes. Adults with refugee status may begin employment as soon as they arrive in the US. Shortly after moving to Illinois, Benga started taking beginners' ESL classes and was hired to assist in the kitchen of a nursing home.

Resettlement organizations often place refugees from the same linguistic and cultural backgrounds in the same area. Doing so helps create a community of newcomer and established refugee families with a language and culture in common, and it also allows for efficiency in hiring caseworkers who understand the cultures and languages of major groups that resettle there. Although Kaleb was from Ethiopia and did not speak Tshiluba, he spoke his native language, Amharic, and was fluent in English and also French, the language he used to communicate with Benga and Dibenesha. The Office of Refugee Resettlement has different arrangements for state-level provision of federal refugee assistance, with either state government or private-public partnerships responsible for administering various support programs, in collaboration with the nine nonprofit organizations.[6] In addition to government and nonprofit agency support, local coalitions of refugees from the same areas offered community aid and networking. Kaleb introduced Benga to the leaders of African Community Outreach, a group whose purpose is "to help African families and individuals maximize their chances of living well, achieving greater goals and making a difference." Years earlier, when Kaleb arrived in Aurora, members of this collective had helped him adjust to his new life, and now he was helping newcomers do the same. The friendships Benga made with families from the Kasai region, as well as other parts of Africa, were tremendously helpful in her and Dibenesha's adjustment to life in the US.

School

Settler Elementary has been serving an increasing number of English learners from various backgrounds during the past seven years, due to an influx of immigrants and refugees who work in meat processing plants. In response to the growing number of Latinx EL students (currently 45 percent of the student population), six years ago Settler initiated a dual language program in English and Spanish at the preschool level (see "Rafael's Story" for more information), adding a grade level each year until reaching fifth grade. Although Dibenesha is an English learner who speaks a less common first language, and therefore did not enroll in the Spanish/English kindergarten class, she benefits in many ways from Settler's dual language education program. The entire school celebrates bilingualism, biliteracy, and biculturalism, recognizing the knowledge and strengths that students from various language and cultural origins offer. In addition, Ms. Regent, the ELD teacher, is an essential member of the dual language team, collaborating with teachers in English-medium and Spanish-medium instruction to connect language development in both. She also coached general classroom teachers, like Mr. Davies, and cotaught with them as well, modeling best practices in teaching English learners, such as the tools and techniques in *Show, Tell, Build*.[7]

Settler Elementary also stands out for its exceptional track record in identifying culturally and linguistically diverse gifted students. At the time the school began implementing dual language education, it also adopted SEM, which uses a gifted education approach to develop the strengths and talents of every student.[8] SEM's three goals of developing the talents of every child, advanced-level enrichment for all students, and advanced follow-up for students based on their strengths optimize inclusive practices for identifying gifted students and providing them with appropriate programing. Had Dibenesha been at a different school, her talents may not have been recognized.

According to the National Center for Research on Gifted Education, 2 percent of ELs are in gifted programs, in contrast with 7 percent of non-ELs, and this disparity is due primarily to identification procedures. The center recommends universal screening, using assessments that are culturally and linguistically appropriate, including nonverbal assessments, and other means of identification. In addition, it suggests incorporating the student's native language ability and hiring multilingual school psychologists. Just as Ms. Donato told Mr. Davies to keep a log of observations, interactions, and informal assessments, the center recommends making "identification of giftedness an ongoing process rather than a single event."[9] Additional concerns specific to identifying giftedness in English learners arise from the fact that these students don't all arrive at US schools for the first time in kindergarten, nor do they all arrive with a level of English proficiency that enables identification of giftedness. For instance, if Dibenesha had arrived in the US in fourth grade not speaking English, the chances that she would be identified as gifted would be diminished because not all schools follow an SEM model that recommends frequent and repeated screening to "identify students whose talents manifest later." Once identified as gifted, EL students should also be provided with supports for learning in their new language, just as they should have in general instruction.[10]

As described in Dibenesha's story, Mr. Davies has the support of the ELD teacher, Ms. Regent, and the gifted coordinator, Ms. Donato. They frequently plan units together, determining where either teacher can coteach or offer resources to support Dibenesha's understanding of the subject matter and her English language development. To support its English learners, Settler Elementary implemented the One Plus Model—Continuum of Systemic Instructional Support for ELs, which offers practical guidelines for different levels of working together.[11]

Family

Dibenesha came to the US with her mother, a widow. What English learners go through in immigrating to US schools can differ greatly by the composition of their family. Dibenesha had no older siblings to pave the way for her, and no younger ones for her to be responsible for. The African refugee communities in Aurora acted as an extended family for mother and daughter, providing communal events, childcare, practical advice, and encouragement. Although Benga struggled with her job demands, which required her to be available on days and times that conflicted with Dibenesha's needs, their extended family helped fill in the gaps. Benga's own school experiences in the adult ESL class were positive, and her teacher was another source of information and support. And Kaleb checked in on them regularly, well beyond their removal from his caseload after the eight-month initial resettlement period. He was always only a phone call away, and Benga wasn't timid about reaching out when necessary.

Student

Dibenesha was just shy of her third birthday when she witnessed her father's murder. The National Child Traumatic Stress Network recommends that when early childhood trauma occurs, assessment of trauma stress should follow as soon as possible. As formal screening did not happen during her time in the refugee camp nor during her first year in the US, the assessment process became more complicated. When Kaleb told Mr. Davies about the experiences Dibenesha had lived through before enrolling at Settler, Mr. Davies notified the school psychologist, who gave him helpful information about his role in watching for behavioral signs. Paying attention to possible delays in motor or language skills, Mr. Davies saw no immediate cause for concern. To be certain that every type of support would be available to Dibenesha if needed, he also set up a meeting with her future first-grade teacher to share insights, and he arranged for the school psychologist to administer the Post-Traumatic Symptom Inventory for Children (TP-SIC).[12] Dibenesha's life was stable now, and she and Benga drew strength and resilience from their community as well as the staff at HIAS. Now the teachers at Settler Elementary were working together to watch for any future signs of traumatic stress development, and the whole team was ready with a broad and deep safety net of services and resources for effective, culturally, and linguistically responsive treatment if needed. Together, they planned for and celebrated Dibenesha's continuing success.

DIBENESHA'S STORY DISCUSSION QUESTIONS

1. Dibenesha and her mother could only carry a few things from the refugee camp to the US. How were the items they brought useful in their new home, and what do you think made them choose those items?

2. Mr. Davies was a third-year teacher who had no experience teaching refugees. What qualities did Mr. Davies have that helped Dibenesha do well in her first year at Settler Elementary? In what way could a new teacher like Mr. Davies be more effective than a veteran teacher in teaching English learners who are refugees if neither teacher had ever taught these types of students? In what way could a veteran teacher be more effective?
3. Mr. Davies created a welcoming environment for Dibenesha. What were the most important actions he took? What else could he have done?
4. What kind of expectations did other teachers at Settler have for Dibenesha? What effect might their expectations have on her progress?
5. The school faculty saw signs of giftedness in Dibenesha. What were some indicators of potential giftedness? How did Dibenesha's background, as well as her status as an EL student, affect potential identification of giftedness? What barriers are there for EL students to be identified as gifted or participate in gifted education?
6. Because of a small rupture in the support system provided for refugee families in Aurora, some important information and support was not provided to Mr. Davies. What could have been done to avoid that gap in services? What could Mr. Davies have done to find out more about Dibenesha and how to help her succeed?

CHAPTER 3

JOSUÉ'S STORY

JUST BY THE SMELL JOSUÉ knew where to sit. Lunchboxes filled with pork tamales wrapped in banana leaves, covered with shiny foil, lured him to the left corner of the cafeteria. There sat a small group of students who looked like him.

Josué pointed to an empty chair and nodded, eyebrows raised.

"Yeah," a boy responded, his face swiveling upward, expressionless, staring at Josué a few seconds beyond comfortable.

Josué reached into his canvas tote bag and unwrapped his tamale.

"Don't you have a lunchbox?" the tablemate asked.

Josué shook his head and kept eating.

Josué's mother, Teresa, had left her home in Chiapas, Mexico, at eighteen. Until that day, she had never traveled more than fifty miles from where she grew up. Once a dangerous center of revolutionary militias, Chiapas had become a peaceful impoverished region. The wilds of Chiapas were astoundingly picturesque, rocky canyons cloaked in lush greenery, with waterfalls overflowing into pools of limestone-rich waters as blue as glacial lakes.

Teresa grew up in a rural area, about fifteen mountainous miles from the capital of Chiapas, San Cristobal. During childhood, Teresa endured the chaos brought on by insurgence, which wrecked her chance to apply her solid intellect to studies beyond primary grades. All she knew about this grave disadvantage was that she stopped going to school much sooner than she expected. This was a lasting sore point because Teresa loved being a student at the breezy, open-air compound located between her home and San Cristobal. The safety, structure, and consistency of school fostered her wholehearted efforts, which, in turn, led to her success. Every object of this special space was dear to Teresa—the molded plastic chairs with swing-down tablet arms to write on, the Bic pens, the spiral notebooks, and the books. The colorful books. Whenever they received a new book, the children held theirs proudly on display beneath their smiling faces, as if they were showing off diplomas in a graduation class photo.

While still a child, Teresa began working in San Cristobal, selling bracelets in the streets of the open-air public market. The ride there was an uninterrupted series of turns, brake-burning switchbacks, and s-curves that hugged narrow roads with steep drop-offs. Every day the van departed for San Cristobal well before dawn, traveling through the darkest of nights, illuminated by nothing but the moon and stars and one working headlight. In the van, Teresa filled her forearms with handcrafted bracelets, ready to approach tourists shopping at the market. The city of 150,000 residents pulsed with activity. By now, Teresa had become accustomed to the random cacophony of taxis and vans prowling the streets, the gorgeous fragrances of fruits and flowers for sale in the market, the delicious corn-scented tamales cooking over open fires, and the putrid odors emanating from trash piles behind dilapidated colonial buildings.

Shortly after turning seventeen, Teresa met a man, twelve years her senior, who had moved from Chiapas to the United States for a field labor job. During the previous ten years, he had worked his way up to crew chief and put aside enough money to return home for a month during a lull in the harvest. Teresa met him in the dusty streets of San Cristobal on December 11, a date to remember, the day before the Festival of the Virgin of Guadalupe. It was a happy day everywhere. Teresa extended her arm to display her bracelets, and the courtship began. In the three weeks he had left in Chiapas, they fell in love, Teresa thought, and he told her they should be together. Doing that made sense because he had a job for her on the Texas-to-Michigan circuit. Crew chiefs have that kind of power.

Teresa couldn't convince her parents to let her leave with him, so their budding relationship became long distance. When Teresa turned eighteen, though, the choice to join him in the US was entirely hers. With the remittance he wired her, she started setting up her route to Starr County, Texas, stuffed her backpack with her warmest clothes, and said goodbye.

Teresa made the journey mostly by bus, meeting up at the Monterrey terminal with the smuggler she had hired to guide her through the northern Mexican desert and across the border river. Her bus trip had lasted almost a week, with stops here and there for meals, showers, and sleep, and she felt weak by the time the most challenging part of the journey began. Around Monterrey, one by one, about a dozen other migrants joined Teresa and the smuggler, moving north inconspicuously together for days on end, to where the river was narrower and not as deep. It took a few days until the conditions were right for her to attempt a river crossing, with no guards in sight on the darkest of nights. Another guide who partnered with her smuggler helped her avoid the currents and make it to the riverbank in Texas.

A car was waiting for her on the other side of the border, and after checking that the driver's name matched the smuggler's directions, Teresa headed toward Rio Grande City to reunite with the man she intended to marry. Crossing the city limits, Teresa crooked her neck to see the Christmas lights, still up and twinkling in early January. There was so much light. Christmas lights upon streetlights. Houses lit up. The night nearly as bright as day.

Teresa and her man lived in a trailer for the next two months, leaving in March to follow the migrant stream from tomato harvests in the Lower Rio Grande Valley to the blueberry season in Van Buren County, Michigan, in July.[1]

Traveling the circuit left no time for anything but work. And work was hard. Every morning the field workers began at dawn, covered completely with long sleeves, bandanas, and hats to block their skin from the sun, burrs, and pesticides, even in the hottest months of summer. With no breaks in their long days, they kept moving, in a monotonous, painful dance of bending and turning to pick and pack, filling their boxes up to the top and loading them onto the trucks. When Teresa's back ached, basically every day, she took aspirin and kept going. No work, no pay. And even though she was the wife of a crew chief, Teresa had no privileges. In the midst of this new life of constant labor and relocation, when they arrived in Illinois for the blackberry harvest, Teresa found out she was four-months' pregnant with Josué.

Being pregnant while working in the fields contributed to a rise in Teresa's blood pressure and glucose levels. The light, persistent rash on the undersides of her arms, an ever-present reaction to the powdery pesticides the farmers sprayed, turned into a continuous patch of redness, swollen and hot to the touch. She could no longer take aspirin for her pain, and a medical leave was an impossibility. Each week dragged on, and with every month that passed a new complication emerged. On the bright side, the timing of Teresa's pregnancy allowed for regular, free clinic visits through her second trimester. However, when the harvest moved northward around her thirtieth week, so did Teresa and her husband. Josué was born seven weeks later, small but strong.

Teresa and her husband maintained the cycles of following the harvest, finding older members of their migrant community to babysit Josué so they both could work. Three years after Josué's arrival, Gabriela was born, following a pregnancy fraught with even more complications.

Josué's growing family continued traveling along the circuit despite the toll it took on both children. From birth through the second grade, Josué was on the move, but this year his parents had an offer to stay put near Aurora, Illinois, working at a blackberry farm and organic greenhouse. Teresa had been building up the courage to make her desires known.

> "I've been thinking about the job offer at the blackberry farm, *mi amor*," Teresa mentioned nonchalantly while chopping tomatoes for dinner.
>
> "Yeah, what about it?" Josué's father replied, scrolling through his phone as he leaned on the kitchen counter.
>
> "Josué will be starting the third grade this fall. That's when schools make students who are behind repeat the grade."
>
> Josué's father set his phone down.
>
> "So? We don't need to worry about that. Josué's doing OK."
>
> "With us moving to a different state every spring, Josué has been struggling. If we stay in one place for the whole year, I think he can catch up."
>
> Teresa looked up for a reaction, her head tilted and her lips stretched into a tight line, mustering a solicitously piteous smile.
>
> "We can make more money if we keep moving," countered Josué's father, jabbing the air in front of him with his index finger.
>
> "Not that much more," Teresa rebutted. "Plus, Gabriela will begin kindergarten. She needs to get a good start."
>
> "That's just play school, Teresa!"
>
> "No, it's not. Children learn how to read in kindergarten."
>
> "They'll be fine. They'll have a better life if we make more money."
>
> "They'll have a better life if they are educated and don't have to work like we do!" Teresa blurted out, quickly recoiling, frightened by the force of her assertion.
>
> Josué's father whipped his head around and faced Teresa head on. "You'd better be grateful for everything I've done for this family! Because of me, *me*, we have a roof over our head and food on our table." He grabbed Teresa's upper arm and shook her once, with force. "What *you* need to do is keep your head down, your mouth shut, and your hands picking. *I'll* make the decisions."

Teresa didn't bring up staying in Illinois for the next week or two. But as the first day of school got closer, she gently made her case to accept the job offers, one small appeal at a time. At the beginning of August, they moved into a sixty-foot single-wide trailer with two other farmworker families, in a park alongside the Fox River. Everyone shared the kitchen, living room, and two bathrooms, and each family bunked together in their bedroom. Cramming two adults and two children into one room made it hard enough to sleep, but the thin exterior walls let in the rushing sound of the river below, which was not soothing to Teresa.

Now Josué and Gabriela had a permanent address for enrolling at school, and Teresa felt her persistence had been rewarded. On the day she went to enroll them at Settler Elementary, there were "Welcome/Bienvenidos" signs in Spanish and English, a pleasant surprise. Teresa wanted Josué and Gabriela to learn Spanish and English, especially because she was raised speaking Tzotzil and Spanish, rather than her indigenous language, was the language her school had used. She knew that speaking Spanish and English, two languages of influence, would give her children more opportunities in life. When Teresa requested to enroll Gabriela in the dual language kindergarten, she was accepted without question, but Josué's application was rejected.

The dual language teachers at Settler Elementary safeguarded the quality of their program in multiple ways. Sometimes that meant convincing the principal not to hire a teacher whose Spanish proficiency wasn't much higher than the children's. Other times it meant requesting more money for materials in both languages, twice what other classrooms needed. Today, it meant possibly excluding a new third grader whose mother wanted him to learn in two languages. It was his bad luck to arrive in third grade, when all students are expected to measure up to standards.

Third-grade dual language teacher Ms. Lorenzo knew that dual language programs benefited English learners and denying that right to a child felt punitive. It wasn't Josué's fault that his family moved with the harvest, or that his parents' education in Mexico had been limited, or that his vocabulary in English and Spanish was at the bottom of the curve. But the decision wasn't hers to make. She had to convince the program coordinator.

Walking to the meeting, Ms. Lorenzo felt short of breath. Would she say the right things to get the boy accepted? She had no doubt that her dual language class would be best for Josué, but she also needed to consider the program. Dual language classes already were under a microscope—some parents feared their third graders' standardized test scores would be lower than students in English-only classrooms. Would the risk of accommodating a struggling student be worth it? Either way, why did Josué have to carry the burden of the entire program's success?

Ms. Lorenzo entered the classroom of the dual language program coordinator, Mrs. Marin.

"¡Hola! I like how you've decorated your classroom this year! Thanks for meeting with me about Josué," Ms. Lorenzo said.

"You're welcome," replied Mrs. Marin. Ms. Lorenzo smiled and took a seat.

"I reviewed Josué's file last week, and I thought he should be placed in the regular third-grade classroom," Ms. Lorenzo began.

"Yes, that's what I think, too!" Mrs. Marin confirmed.

Ms. Lorenzo continued, "But then Miss Julie asked me to meet with her about it, and now I feel he should be in dual language."

Mrs. Marin leaned forward, letting out a disapproving sigh. The door creaked open.

"Oh, here she is!" Ms. Lorenzo exclaimed. "We were just talking about what you shared with me on Monday."

Miss Julie smiled. "Perfect timing! Nice to meet you, Mrs. Marin!"

Mrs. Marin nodded.

Miss Julie walked over, sat down, and continued, "Last week I did a home visit and talked with Josué and his mother. Josué speaks English and Spanish equally well, and his mother is very committed to him learning both languages. Josué told me he wants to be in a dual language classroom—he said it twice, once in English, and once in Spanish."

"Uh . . . but his reading scores are on a first-grade level, and he's never been in a Spanish-speaking classroom," said Mrs. Marin. "Migrant kids who aren't proficient in any language aren't right for dual language programs."

Mrs. Marin moved toward Miss Julie and shook her index finger. "I appreciate your input, Miss Julie, but you're a social worker, not a teacher."

Ms. Lorenzo froze, waiting for Miss Julie's response.

"Actually, I was just hired as a migrant advocate, first one Settler's ever had. And I *am* a teacher, with a master's degree in bilingual education," Miss Julie responded calmly. "We all know the research—dual language programs have better outcomes for English learners. I don't think we should worry about the reputation of the program more than the best interests of a child."

Ms. Lorenzo took a deep breath before speaking. "I know Josué's behind, but I'll work with him. I'll spend extra time with him and help him catch up. Why start with no before we give it a try?"

"I'll help, too" offered Miss Julie. "And I'm sure Ms. Regent will provide a lot of support."

Mrs. Marin shook her head. "I'll leave it up to you, Ms. Lorenzo. But I think it's a very bad idea."

There they were—the famous talking walls. Ms. Lorenzo's classroom looked like a 3M chart-paper factory had had a sneezing fit. Little slivers of painted drywall peeked through the gaps in the floor-to-ceiling educational wallpapering that Ms. Lorenzo had put up for her new class. English in blue, Spanish in red, the charts displayed the steps in writing a paragraph, solving a multiplication problem, using the scientific method, and much, much more. Most had colorful clip art and photos, too. No place else in the world looked like Ms. Lorenzo's third-grade dual language classroom.

Ms. Lorenzo called roll one by one, and when she got to Josué, she said, *ho-su-way*'. She actually said it right, not *José* like the teachers from the many towns where he had gone to school. Josué remembered the taunts of "no way, José" that his former classmates lobbed at him like a grenade whenever the teacher said his name. By the time he finished kindergarten, he had grown tired of correcting the multitude of mispronouncers and just let it go.

As Ms. Lorenzo modeled the first classroom rule, "morning procedures," in Spanish, Josué paid close attention. "Hang your backpack on a hook," she said while demonstrating the action. "Place your lunchbox in the bin," she continued with the next four steps of starting the day. Then, she selected a volunteer to read the rules aloud from the red-lettered chart-paper list she had prepared. After each step was read, a different student demonstrated the action. Josué watched and listened, secure in his understanding of what to do when he arrived at school.

While her students were at recess, Ms. Lorenzo made a file to document the one-on-one and small group support she planned for Josué. She reviewed the printouts of his test scores and started listing the tiered support she would provide him. Seeing that his reading skills were below grade level in both languages, she would have to give equal focus to English and Spanish. Reading independently on a first-grade level was not a good way to start third grade, but other students had made big gains with targeted support, so why not Josué?

After walking back with her class from the playground to their room, Ms. Lorenzo pulled Josué aside. She pointed to his backpack, frayed at the seams and stained on the bottom, hanging properly on the hook with his name above it.

"See this?" she asked.

Josué nodded.

"Tomorrow, I want you to bring it to school empty and give it to me. I'm going to fill it with important things."

On her way home that afternoon, Ms. Lorenzo stopped at a warehouse that stored items from the local school supply drive. She quickly grabbed an assortment of pencils—#2, mechanical, and colored—a pencil sharpener, a plastic pencil box, an oversized pink eraser, glue sticks, safety scissors, three spiral notebooks, and a box of twenty-four crayons. That was it for now, as any more wouldn't fit in Josué's empty pack.

Since filling Josué's backpack the week before, Ms. Lorenzo coaxed him to sit and talk with her during lunch. During their previous interactions, she had done all the talking, and now she wanted to hear from him. So far, he hadn't volunteered to answer questions in class. She actually never recalled hearing the sound of his voice.

Josué walked up to Ms. Lorenzo's desk.

"What did you bring for lunch, Josué?"

Josué peeled back the foil around a tamale.

"That looks delicious. ¿Te gustan los tamales?"

Josué nodded and smiled.

"Do you have something to drink? Where's your lunchbox?"

Josué held up his tote bag and pulled out a juice box.

"Is that your lunchbox? Where did you get that?"

"At the church office."

Ms. Lorenzo knew what he meant. She had donated "gently worn" clothes and other items to the Interfaith Farmworker Support Cooperative that her synagogue and a local church ran. This was the first time that one of those donations made it to her classroom. The tote bag that her husband was handed when he registered for a work conference was now Josué's lunchbox, a poor insulator for Teresa's homemade tamales, but its silk-screened logo, *IAMP: Individually Proud, Collectively Strong*, seemed to imply something grander than a corporate slogan.

Ms. Lorenzo continued in Spanish.

"That's my favorite color, blue. What's your favorite color?"

"Verde," Josué responded decisively.

"Nice. Great color! Oh yeah, bring me that empty backpack Wednesday morning. I'll have some more good things to put in it."

When she went grocery shopping that evening, she bought Josué a dark green insulated lunchbox and filled it with Goldfish packets and granola bars. She stopped by the school supply warehouse the next afternoon and found a new backpack in almost the same shade of green, which she used as a shopping basket as she combed the aisles for Josué's remaining necessities.

Miss Julie came in at 5:30 a.m. every day, on her own time, to open up her oversized office for migrant students whose parents went to work before dawn. Settler Elementary's before-school program started an hour after Miss Julie arrived, and the $30 registration fee plus a $12-a-week charge per child was out of reach for the families of students like Josué and Gabriela, so she organized and oversaw a study hall in her office until the morning bell rang.

"¡Hola niños! ¿Cómo están?" Miss Julie greeted the children at the drop-off zone.

"Gabriela, I have some fun activities for you this morning while I work with Josué."

Gabriela giggled and smiled.

"All you kindergartners will be at your center, and the rest of you will work with the computers until I call on you."

Once the children were settled in her office, Miss Julie sat down next to Josué. The day before she had reviewed the results of a bilingual informal reading assessment that Ms. Lorenzo gave Josué. She noticed that he had inconsistencies in sounding out words in both languages and that he struggled with describing key ideas and details about what he read. Although these were possible signs of a learning disability or language disorder, Miss Julie thought it could just as likely be a result of his interrupted schooling. Their time together every day would help find out which it was.

So, each morning, she set aside thirty minutes for Josué, and she also arranged for a bilingual high school student to tutor him after school and on

Saturdays. Using the activities Miss Julie made, Josué and the tutor read many fiction and nonfiction books aloud in both languages and discussed the chapters and their meaning. They also worked regularly on building Josué's vocabulary, focusing on words that were similar in both languages, something they both learned are called *cognates*.

One morning, when Miss Julie took her third graders to Ms. Lorenzo's class, she asked if they could speak for a minute.

> "Sure! What's up?" Ms. Lorenzo asked as she stepped into the hallway, holding her classroom door slightly open behind her back.
>
> "Josué's been improving his reading slowly. I'm happy he's progressing, but it's taking longer than the amount of time he has to catch up," said Miss Julie.
>
> "I know, I've used second-tier interventions for reading with him so far, but I plan to start tier-three support next week," Ms. Lorenzo responded.
>
> "That extra attention should help. We'll see how he responds," said Miss Julie.
>
> Ms. Lorenzo started to push her classroom door farther open, turning slowly toward it.
>
> "Ms. Lorenzo, there's something else I noticed about Josué," Miss Julie said quickly.
>
> "What?" Ms. Lorenzo asked, concerned. "Do you think there's a disability?"
>
> "Oh. No. Um . . . ," Ms. Julie hesitated for a moment, surprised by the question. "Actually, maybe, but not a *learning* disability. More like an impairment, really."
>
> "Go on," said Ms. Lorenzo.
>
> "I've been noticing that Josué squints a lot. Since I work with him so early in the morning, I also see him rubbing his eyes, so I thought he might just be sleepy. But it could be a vision problem. Have you noticed any squinting?"
>
> "Now that you mention it, I *have* noticed him squinting," Ms. Lorenzo confirmed.
>
> "Well then, I'll see if I can get him an appointment with an optometrist," Miss Julie said.
>
> "Sounds good. Keep me posted," Ms. Lorenzo responded as she returned to her noisy class.

The next week Miss Julie took Josué to the eye doctor, who determined he needed glasses. Because he and Miss Julie were childhood friends, the optometrist didn't charge for the visit, and he even donated the glasses, letting Josué pick from the moderately priced options.

Soon after, Miss Julie took Josué and Gabriela to her own dentist, who offered her service pro bono—the first time they'd had their teeth checked. After the cleaning, brother and sister flashed their toothiest smiles proudly for a selfie Miss Julie took of the trio.

Now that the bracing chill of winter had overtaken Aurora, the children in Miss Julie's before-school care were constantly talking about the upcoming Las Posadas procession that the Iglesia de San Pedro de Jesús Maldonado had organized. One first grader's older sister was portraying Mary, and a fourth grader's big brother was going to be Joseph, and all of Miss Julie's students planned to participate. The early morning gatherings were becoming more animated and festive as December 16 approached, and Miss Julie felt an urgency to tie up loose ends before the break.

Miss Julie had been in regular contact with Gabriela's teacher, and the reports were always outstanding. Gabriela was right on target in both languages, a very bright and inquisitive girl. Ms. Lorenzo had been meeting every other week with Miss Julie, and at this point they both were quite pleased with Josué's gains. In four months, he had made one year's progress in reading, and with his corrected eyesight, he was becoming an eager reader of nonfiction. Ms. Lorenzo guided him to books about dinosaurs, sports legends, racecars, and other topics of fascination, and Josué was asking for more.

After the joyful diversions of the holidays, as the spring months approached, Josué's father decided that the family would leave their home and follow the harvest again. Besides the money, he missed traveling, as he had "friends" in each of the towns they stopped in, and he liked to go out to see them and have a good time all hours of the night. He found that staying in one place was boring, and he hated the cold weather and overcast skies that seemed to last forever in Aurora.

As Teresa heard these new plans for the first time, so did Josué, who awakened upon hearing his parents' raised voices. They usually argued in Tzotzil to keep the kids from understanding, but that night his father was screaming in Spanish. Teresa countered with the same points she made in the summer, but it got her nowhere. She tried to stay calm to keep the volume down, but when Josué's father said he was planning to get Josué prepared to start working with him in the summer, she could hold back no longer.

Teresa told him how selfish he had been, always putting himself first and his children last. She told him that Josué wasn't going to work in the fields, and Gabriela wasn't going to marry young and quit school, like he always said she would. She told him that she constantly felt so alone, even when she was at his side, in the fields or at home, and that her only goal in life was to make her children's lives better than hers. The fear that kept her quiet for years was eclipsed by her current anger, which over time had come to fruition, and as she spoke the truth of her experience, her husband stood there, shocked and blank-faced.

Once done talking, she looked her husband square in the eyes for a few long seconds, waiting silently for a response. He stared back at her for an instant, then he turned, grabbed his truck keys, and left.

On Saturday, like every other weekend since she began working at Settler, Miss Julie was back at the migrant farmworker trailer park in a van with Wi-Fi hot spots, so the children who lived there could do homework and meet with tutors online. Normally Josué and Gabriela ran to meet her, helping set up her folding table and chairs, but today she did that task alone. When they didn't show up by the time she had to leave, she stopped by their trailer and peeked inside. One of the other occupants told her Josué and his family had moved out early that morning.

Miss Julie got back in the van and called Teresa. Miss Julie stayed silent while Teresa told the whole story, reliving the history of her family's relocation to Aurora and her abject state of panic about what's next, ending with the hard fact that she, Josué, and Gabriela had to move into a nearby motel, but it would be for just two days because they only had enough money to pay for the weekend. They were, by all definitions, homeless.

Miss Julie drove to an extended-stay motel and paid for the next week in advance with emergency funds that the Farmworker Cooperative collected, and she immediately began searching for a long-term solution. She looked up trailer parks in the area and found a nice one whose residents were mainly retirees, so she drove straight over to take a look before dark. The park manager told her how much monthly lot rent cost, which was actually very reasonable, and he said a couple trailers were currently for sale. There was a turnkey one that cost $20,000, which she told him was more than her budget allowed, but then he remembered that a fixer-upper had just gone on the market for $8,000. Julie asked to look inside, and, as she expected, it was in pretty bad shape. But Julie had an eye for renovation and redecoration, and thought it had potential.

On the drive home, her initial enthusiasm waned as she realized that even an $8,000 home was out of reach for Teresa and her two kids. She couldn't get it out of her mind, though, and even drove around her block a few times before pulling into her driveway so she could give it more thought.

"How'd your day go, Julie?" her husband Bruce asked as she walked into the kitchen.

"Uhh . . ." she sighed. "It was tough."

"I'm sorry, honey."

Miss Julie sighed again, then continued, hesitatingly.

"You know, Bruce, we've been saving part of our paychecks for that Mediterranean cruise for a while."

"Yeah, we're up to around $7,000. Pretty good, right? I bet you're ready for a relaxing cruise after today!" Bruce leaned back and pantomimed chilling on a chaise lounge by the pool.

"Well, you know what I would enjoy more than a Mediterranean cruise?" Miss Julie asked.

Bruce looked on, intrigued.

"I would enjoy buying and making over an old trailer that will be a great home for one of my migrant families." Miss Julie peered at Bruce with an *I-know-this-sounds-crazy* expression, then continued.

"I found out this morning that the mom and her two elementary-aged children are living in a motel, and I spent the afternoon looking for a permanent place for them."

An awkward silence followed. Julie tilted her head and raised her eyebrows. Bruce returned her expression and held it for a bit. Then he smiled. "That sounds like a wonderful vacation, Julie. I'm in."

So, together they organized an alternative spring break renovation project for a group of fifteen parochial school students, raised additional funds and donations from the Farmworker Cooperative, and spent every dollar of their vacation fund in a way that made them happier than any trip.

When Miss Julie drove Teresa, Josué, and Gabriela to their new home, it already looked from the outside as if a TV makeover show had remodeled the place.

Miss Julie ceremoniously unlocked the front door, and Gabriela began to look around for other residents.

> "There's no one else here," said Miss Julie.
>
> "Is this whole trailer ours?" asked Gabriela.
>
> "Yes, and you have your very own room. Let's go see it!"

As the children worked their way through the living room, kitchen, two bathrooms, and hallway, they walked on just-installed linoleum floors, saw brightly painted walls, flushed new toilets that didn't keep running, smiled at themselves in the stainless-steel kitchen appliances, and turned on cooling and heating wall units in each room. But the best part of all was a mermaid-themed bedroom for Gabriela, and a Lego-themed room for Josué, both with proper desks for studying and shelves filled with books in Spanish and English. Teresa's bedroom was nearby, at the end of the hall, decorated in soothing tones of blue that reminded her of the waterfalls of Chiapas.

There was a bit of a ruckus right in front of the stage. A dozen third graders had gathered in a huddle, oohing and aahing over an intricate, shoebox-sized dragon made of Legos. Josué carefully handed it to the first person in the group, who began passing it around for all to see and touch.

> "It must have taken you a long time to put this together, Josué," one of his classmates said.
>
> "Not too long," Josué replied. "I've got some other cool Lego sets we can put together when you come over on Sunday."
>
> "I can't wait!" Josué's friend exclaimed.
>
> "I wanna come, too!" said another classmate.
>
> Josué stood up a bit straighter and smiled.
>
> "Sure! Our moms can talk when they get here," Josué offered confidently.

The lunchroom was filling up quickly, and everyone was settling into their seats. School would be out for the summer in a few days, and this afternoon was all about celebration. Student awards were being handed out, and no one knew who would get to go on stage and accept theirs.

Like a college graduation, the event began with a guest speaker, a professor of Mayan origin from Mexico who was part of an exchange program at Aurora University. "Like some of you, I come from indigenous roots in Latin America," she told the fidgety crowd. "And even if I was the only one who believed in me, I was determined to work hard to make it to college and study physics, my passion. And here I am now, a professor with over fifty publications, who was born and raised in a small town in Chiapas."

Josué perked up at hearing his family's region and high-fived a classmate whose mother was from there, too.

When the professor finished, Ms. Lorenzo climbed the steps onto the stage and took the microphone, addressing the audience in Spanish, then English.

"I'm so happy to welcome all of the families who came to celebrate today. We are honoring Settler's students' achievements, and we just heard from a distinguished scholar from Mexico, reflecting Latin American pride."

A collective cheer rose from the floor.

"Many of you don't know this, but I came here from South America with my husband, two daughters, and eight suitcases. That's it. All we had left in the world was what we carried with us, and, you know, that could be taken from us, too. I was sure, though, that no one could ever take my most valuable possession. My brain! I have it with me always, and I use it all the time."

The crowd laughed.

"So, I tell my students, you might have had to move from place to place, and maybe you don't have much to call your own, but just like me, you have your brains, and you will make them stronger and smarter at school. And most of all, hold your head high and be proud of who you are and what you accomplish.

"And now, I'm delighted to present the awards to our third-grade students."

Ms. Lorenzo called one little girl up to receive the math award, then another for the science one. Next came reading.

"And the reading achievement award goes to . . ." Ms. Lorenzo let the suspense build. "Josué López!"

Josué jumped to his feet.

"Come on up, Josué!"

Josué ran up the stairs and hugged Ms. Lorenzo.

"Josué worked really hard this year, and he did something pretty amazing. He made time speed up. Yes, he put two-and-a-half years of accomplishment into one year of school. I'm so proud of him!"

The cheering and applause delighted Josué, who lifted his arms above his head and pointed skyward, like an Olympic athlete who had won the hundred-meter dash.

Ms. Marin met Josué at the bottom of the steps, congratulating him and letting him know she was looking forward to having him in her fourth-grade class next fall. Then, his classmates stopped him for fist bumps as he made his way toward Ms. Lorenzo. Teresa had already spotted her and was on her way there, too.

"Señora Lorenzo," said Teresa in Spanish, "these are for you."

Teresa pushed a bag overfilled with gorgeous fresh tomatoes and bell peppers into Ms. Lorenzo's hands.

"We grow these at the greenhouse."

"They are the most perfect produce I've ever seen. Thank you so much for this wonderful gift," Ms. Lorenzo said.

"They put me in charge of grafting. No more traveling, no more heavy lifting." Teresa smiled.

"I'm so happy for you and your family, Teresa."

Miss Julie walked up and started taking group selfies.

"Teresa, we are all so proud of Josué. He did it!" Miss Julie exclaimed.

Ms. Lorenzo headed back to her empty classroom, energized and content. She set her things down on her desk, admiring once more the tomatoes and peppers that tumbled out of the sack. A couple of books she had been carrying lay on top of the bag, so she picked them up to file on her shelves. Underneath she noticed something familiar. "Individually Proud. Collectively Strong," the blue canvas tote bag proclaimed. Ms. Lorenzo paused and took a deep breath.

She gathered the rest of the produce and put it in the crate of papers that she took home to grade every night. Then she pinned the bag on her wall, logo displayed. The famous walls were getting ready for next year, with a new class motto as their centerpiece.

EPILOGUE

Birth Home (or Family's Place of Origin) to US Home

Mexico is home to 128 million residents. It is a federal presidential republic, and its capital is Mexico City. With a climate that ranges from arid desert to tropical rainforest, its land area covers almost 2 million square kilometers. If superimposed on the US landmass, Mexico's length would extend from the Canada-US border to the state line of Florida. Approximately 80 percent of Mexico's population lives in urban areas, and the major ethnicity is Amerindian Spanish, at 62 percent. About 6 percent of the population speaks indigenous languages.[2]

Mexico is home to sixty-eight different indigenous groups. There are 11 language families, from which 364 dialects are spoken.[3] In general, the older the person, the more likely an indigenous language is their mother tongue, with 11 percent of children ages zero to four and 27 percent of adults age seventy-five and above speaking an indigenous first language.[4] Seventy percent of Mexico's indigenous population lives in poverty. Indigenous women, in particular, have been denied rights and opportunities, resulting in the highest illiteracy and school dropout rates, joblessness, and instances of domestic violence in Mexico.[5]

Mexico is bordered by Guatemala and Belize to the south, and the United States to the north, with coastal areas on the Pacific Ocean, Caribbean Sea, and Gulf of Mexico. The Chiapas region of Mexico is its southernmost area, which borders Central America. Many asylum seekers from Guatemala, Honduras, and Nicaragua leave home to escape gang violence, natural disasters, and government corruption and instability, making their way north through the border between Guatemala and Chiapas.[6]

Although Teresa was not a Central American asylum applicant, she has much in common with them. Like many Guatemalan citizens, most of the people from Chiapas are of Mayan origin.[7] Additionally, Teresa's experience entering the United States was similar to many Central Americans' journey north. As an undocumented resident of the US, Teresa lacked numerous protections and rights and was vulnerable to exploitation. She was, however, an adult when entering, which is not the case for countless desperate Central American children and teens, some of whom make their way to the US without their parents or adult relatives.[8] Although Mexico's government policies toward migrants from the south have resulted in increased detentions at the border in Chiapas, many of the Mexican people provide shelter, food, and other essential needs to Central Americans traveling through Mexico to the US. There are a number of *albergues* (shelters for migrants) in Chiapas run by churches and community organizations.[9]

The ancient Mayans are known for achievements in astronomy, agriculture, engineering, and communications. They created a complex written language, developed two intricate calendar systems, built lasting pyramids that aligned with seasonal events, and cultivated a variety of crops under barren conditions.[10] The Mayans also made contributions to math and science, having invented the concept of zero, independently of the Mesopotamians, around 350 AD.[11] Mayan descendants carry on many traditions of the ancient peoples.[12] Students of Mayan origin have a distinguished history to be proud of, and teachers can make connections between Mayan contributions and current school subjects to nurture cultural pride and a sense of belonging.

Community in the United States

Americans of Mexican origin have long been part of the history of the United States, and generations of Mexican American communities have been established in different regions of the US. In Josué's case, he and his family are part of a first-generation immigrant family from Mexico who happen to be migrant farmworkers.

Migrant farmworkers are the backbone of American agriculture. Some farmworkers enter the US through a limited seasonal worker option, called the H-2A Temporary Agricultural Workers program.[13] Certain conditions must be met for approval, so farmers that may not be eligible to solicit workers from this program elect to hire undocumented workers instead.[14] Labor practices for farmworkers are insufficiently regulated, and working conditions may be harsh, especially for those who are in the US without documents, as they have no legal recourse for abuse or criminal activity for fear of being detained and deported. According to Farmworker Justice, agricultural workers lack basic workplace rights, and the few rights they do have are often unenforced.[15] Their wages are low and do not require adherence to minimum wage laws if they are paid by the piece, which is common, and their working conditions are dangerous, with high incidences of workplace injuries and physical ailments from exposure to toxic chemicals. Seventy-one percent of farmworkers are foreign born, with the vast majority coming from Mexico and Central America. There are half a million children who work in agriculture in the US.

Any teacher knows the importance of consistent attendance in achieving academic success. The children of migrant workers face not only the challenges of poverty but also the demands of moving from school to school with the harvest, creating absences and discontinuity of instruction. The moving, real-life story of José M. Hernández, "farmworker turned astronaut," shows the impact of teachers in the lives of children from farmworker families.[16] José was born to a migrant farming family that traveled from Mexico to follow the harvest, from southern California north to Stockton, California, every March through November. Concerned about wasting the potential of a smart, dedicated student, Miss Egg, José's elementary teacher in Stockton, convinced his parents to settle there and helped them find jobs and housing. José went on to excel in science, eventually earning a degree in electrical engineering. He had always dreamed of becoming an astronaut, so he prepared for and applied to be part of the US Space Shuttle corps. His application was rejected, but rather than giving up, he prepared harder and applied again. The second time was not the charm, and he continued to build new skills and knowledge with each rejection, until he was accepted to the nineteenth class of astronauts in 2004, his thirteenth attempt. In 2009, he was a crew member on the STS-128 mission of the *Space Shuttle Discovery*. One of his honored guests at Kennedy Space Center, who watched him soar into space, was Miss Egg, the teacher who believed in him.

School

The stories have shown that the teachers, administrators, and staff of Settler Elementary are proud of its dual language program. They follow established principles for quality dual language education, but sometimes circumstances dictate deviation from preferred criteria, such as with Josué's first-time enrollment in a dual language program in the third grade.[17] Typically, students are encouraged to enroll in dual language immersion programs from the earliest grade the program is available (usually prekindergarten or kindergarten) and to continue in the program until its highest grade (ideally through high school). Dual language immersion programs sometimes restrict when and which new students can join the program, with cutoffs in second grade or earlier unless students can demonstrate sufficient proficiency in both languages. Because of the contested history of bilingual education in the United States, a great deal of research has been conducted to ascertain the effectiveness of dual language immersion, a more recent type of bilingual education. Researchers have found that these programs enable English learners to close the achievement gap on standardized tests, and in addition, they have the benefit of becoming bilingual, biliterate, and bicultural.[18]

Because there was concern that perhaps something other than gaps in schooling was affecting Josué's progress, Ms. Lorenzo used a system of monitored interventions called Multi-Tiered System of Support, or MTSS.[19] The idea behind MTSS is to provide a continuum of instructional support for all students, with increasing levels of support for those who are struggling. Students' response to support is gauged by various forms of data, including formal and informal assessment. Happily, Josué responded well to the instructional support over time, and there was no need to refer him for potential identification of a learning disability or a speech-language disorder.

Helping Josué reach grade-level proficiency reduced his risk of becoming a long-term English learner (LTEL).[20] There are many students who began school in the US in kindergarten, like Josué, who are still classified as English learners in fifth grade and beyond. Ms. Lorenzo had previously taught fifth grade and saw how students who had not been reclassified from English learner to former English learner by that point were falling further behind. Keeping expectations high and providing the support to reach them was her approach for English learners in every grade.

Settler Elementary was fortunate to have a migrant advocate, a federally funded position.[21] Miss Julie provided a trove of resources and services for students from migrant farmworker families, going beyond limited federal funding to seek donations of time and goods. Just before the school year began, she convinced a local business that had upgraded its computers to donate the old ones to her unofficial before-school program, and every week she drove to the airport to pick up leftover snack packets from two major airlines so she could make sure the children had something to eat if they got hungry at school. Miss Julie's parents had fled Cuba in the early 1960s, starting over in Florida, where they built happy and successful lives. Miss Julie has been giving back to this country and its new residents her entire life.

Family

Some might wonder why all immigrant families don't follow legal procedures for coming to the US, but in the case of Mexican citizens like Josué's parents, there are few options. For example, while another student's family in this book was able to immigrate because of the visa lottery, people from Mexico are not eligible.[22] Similarly, another student's family was able to move to the US legally because they had close family members in the US who owned a successful business that promised to employ them, but Teresa had no such affordances.

Josué's family had no relatives or friends to help them financially, so they were constantly one setback away from calamity. This made them dependent on the honesty, integrity, and generosity of their employers, who varied greatly in those virtues. Teresa's permanent employer in Aurora treated her fairly and professionally, giving her the chance for advancement and increased pay. This had a profound effect on her and her children's well-being.

Josué's story showed that Settler's dual language program was beneficial for him and Gabriela, but it was beneficial for Teresa as well. Because the children were learning in both languages, Teresa could help with homework in Spanish, and the connection the teachers made between the two languages, called *bridging*, helped Teresa learn basic English while helping her children acquire their second language, too.

Teresa's new job grafting plants in the greenhouse provided opportunities to get to know her coworkers and to develop friendships and networks of support. Although she was a single mother, and her family was thousands of miles away, she met and formed friendships with other moms and families at work, church, and school events, so she didn't feel so alone anymore.

Student

When Josué began attending Settler Elementary, he was shy and didn't talk. A number of factors contributed to his initial reticence and disengagement. Of course, self-consciousness about his English proficiency had an effect on his willingness to speak. So did his secondhand clothes and supplies, which provoked belittling questions and stares. Not seeing well affected his reading, which made it difficult to answer the teacher's comprehension questions or discuss stories with classmates. And lack of dental care suppressed his smile. On top of everything, he worried about leaving in the middle of the year and feeling the loss more deeply if he put his whole heart and mind into this new school. As Ms. Lorenzo, Miss Julie, and Teresa worked together to address each of these issues, Josué became more confident about just being himself.

Until Josué's family got their own home, he never had friends come to visit. Now Josué invited friends from school over every week. He also got to know some of the retirees at the trailer park, who helped him with homework now and then and bought him and Gabriela books for birthdays and other special occasions.

JOSUÉ'S STORY DISCUSSION QUESTIONS

1. On the first day of school, Josué gravitated toward kids from similar cultural backgrounds in the lunchroom. Do you think these groupings should occur naturally, or does the school have a role to play in forming students' social connections? What are the more positive or less positive aspects of any students' friendships with schoolmates from similar backgrounds?
2. Teresa's immigration story was sparked by her love for and trust in Josué's father. Do you know anyone who moved to another country because of love? How was their story similar to or different from Teresa's? How did gender affect the process and outcomes?
3. Josué's family moved with the harvest for many years. Families often have to move for work, and their children have to adapt to new schools and communities. How is the life of a migrant farmworker family similar to and different from other families that move frequently, such as military families or families with parents that are relocated by their company or other career opportunities?
4. The dual language coordinator, Ms. Marin, only wanted to admit academically strong students in the upper grades. When schools implement special programs that hold promise for improving achievement for all

students, is it ever right to exclude some students? If so, under what circumstances would you recommend exclusivity and why?

5. Ms. Lorenzo's attitude is to consider trying something outside of the rules before automatically saying no. What are the pros and cons of this position? If you were her, would you have agreed to admit Josué to your class and provide extra support? Why or why not?
6. It took a very dedicated person like Miss Julie, who had a unique job as migrant advocate, to take care of issues that were affecting Josué's schoolwork, such as getting him glasses and dental care. In your option, to what degree should the school be involved in these types of nonacademic concerns? Do you see this as a matter of promoting equity and/or family responsibility, or some of both?
7. With all the support from many professionals and volunteers, Josué was able to reach grade-level proficiency in the third grade. Ms. Lorenzo always says that education is a team sport. Do you agree with her? Why or why not? How have you been a team player, and what were the results?
8. To foster students' achievement, educators at Settler Elementary encouraged them to be proud of their heritage. Besides the convocation speeches about being proud of their cultures, what did Settler and its teachers do to promote pride in their English learners? What else could they do to instill pride and high expectations? What have you done to accomplish this with your students or within your community?

CHAPTER 4

ANH'S STORY

THE SCHOOL BUS had no air-conditioning. Even though it was still morning, the muggy August heat made the middle schoolers feel like they were riding across town in a pressure cooker. Anh pulled her limbs and possessions in tight, shrinking the space she occupied on the padded vinyl seat. At the next stop, two boys jumped on, filing past the first few half-occupied rows with an air of teenage discernment. Anh kept her gaze downward, interrupted only briefly by a quick, side-eye glimpse as the boys walked past her to the back.

By the time they pulled away from the last stop, Anh realized that she knew absolutely no one on the bus. Although she had attended an elementary school in the same zone, there was not one familiar face.

Anh's father, Tranh, was the youngest of four. Tranh's oldest brother, Bao, escaped Vietnam in 1980, jammed together with ninety-six other refugees on a sixty-foot fishing boat, making its way across the South China Sea to a refugee camp in Malaysia.

Once resettled in Florida, Bao got a job as a back-of-the-house porter at a big theme park hotel, inching his way up to maintenance journeyman over the next few years. As he learned to make small repairs and replacements, he also tucked away about a quarter of his salary, which he used to put a down payment on a fixer-upper duplex in a declining neighborhood on the edge of downtown Orlando.

Living in one apartment and renting the other, Bao soon welcomed his new wife into their small home, which felt even smaller within a year, as their family was expanding. Despite more mouths to feed, he and his wife continued to save part of their salaries and began investing in rental properties that eventually they both were able to maintain and manage full-time. This business evolved into a successful property rental company, with ten full-time employees.

At Bao's encouragement, in 2013 his brother Tranh and Tranh's wife, Hong, brought Anh and her younger sister, Hien, from their home in Hue City, Vietnam, to the United States on a tourist visa, which they extended to its legal time limit so Anh could attend kindergarten for an entire school year. Tranh and

Hong had saved for this prolonged trip, but the small sum tided them over during their stay only because Bao invited them to live with his family, by now residing in a considerably larger house than his starter home. A sizable assemblage of Vietnamese families had made Orlando home, and Bao and his wife had become the community's leading real estate experts, with a prominent office on Colonial Drive, the main artery of the city's Little Vietnam.

Anh's tourist experience in kindergarten had been mainly positive, and she and her family took to their lives in Central Florida with relative ease. She made steady progress in learning English, and by the end of the year, when it was time to return to Vietnam, Anh sounded almost like the children who were born in the Sunshine State. Seeing Anh's advancement at school, and wanting the same for her little sister, Tranh and Hong decided that once they were back in Hue City, they would start the process for emigrating to the US.

As Tranh and Hong compiled the reams of documents for their application in Vietnam, Bao worked the western front to get Tranh's family to the US. His successful business allowed him to promise them a comfortable livelihood preparing properties in between tenants, a plus in the family reunification visa application process. Although they met all criteria for acceptance, Tranh's family did not receive approval for five years. In two weeks' time, they packed eight suitcases, said their goodbyes, and ventured off into their new American lives.

"Remember that?" Bao asked Anh.

"Disney World!" she shouted as they carried their luggage past the ubiquitous billboards in the terminal. "How soon can we go?"

"You're lucky you have a cousin who works there, so we'll see when she can get us in."

Anh remembered how much fun she had when she was five, posing for photos with princesses and eating turkey legs.

"I want to watch the fireworks!" Ahn exclaimed, meaning their next visit would last until the monorails stopped running. She recalled all the sensory delights, eager to relive them.

"Oh, there's the eye!" she exclaimed as the minivan sped past Orlando's Ferris wheel, rimmed in color-changing neon lights. "Will we go past my old school on the way home?"

"No, they changed the road from Orlando International," replied Uncle Bao as he glimpsed Anh's disappointed expression in the rearview mirror.

"I wanna go back and see it."

"Maybe next week," Bao responded.

Anh thought back to her kindergarten days, to the pulpy texture of construction paper, the rubber-ducky scent of play fruit and vegetables, and the dragging squeaks of magic markers printing letters with care. She remembered sitting on the round rug and on miniature molded-plastic chairs, and hanging her flimsy backpack on its designated hook.

The headlights of Uncle Bao's minivan illuminated the front yard of the duplex as he turned onto the driveway. Anh peered through the backseat window at the simple concrete block ranch home with a low-pitch roof. Once inside, they all toured the house methodically, with Bao pointing out its features, Realtor style.

"Which room is mine?" Anh asked after noticing there were three bedrooms.

"We'll need some time to decide," Tranh responded.

Anh walked right past the room she wanted, heading to the backyard.

"Where's the pool?" she asked.

Bao started, "There's no . . ."

Tranh quickly interjected, abashedly, "We can go swimming when we visit Uncle Bao. Just think how much you are going to enjoy having your own room."

That did sound good to Anh, especially because in Vietnam she had to share a room with Hien. She walked back to her preferred room, stepped inside, and started visualizing it fully furnished and decorated to tween taste.

The next two weeks passed quickly, topped off with a day at the animal-themed Disney park to celebrate the end of summer break. Anh's cousin helped take care of the giraffes as part of a veterinary internship, and she had stashed away some free passes for the family.

Anh and her family met her cousin during her lunch break and got to see the animal care center where she worked. It was a steamy August day, so a few minutes behind the scenes, enjoying the air-conditioning, gave them a boost to stay till the end. Anh took careful note of her cousin's khaki scout-style uniform and engraved name tag.

"Are you excited to be here, Anh?"

"Yes!"

"What are you most excited about?" her cousin asked, expecting something to do with the theme parks.

"Going to school," Anh replied. "I remember how much fun school is in Florida."

"Make sure you stay to the right when you get off the bus!" Anh had barely arrived at school and she was already being yelled at. "OK," she confirmed timidly, as she walked between the folding yellow doors and faced the sprawling campus of Chevron Middle School.

Anh's first class was social studies with Mrs. McNamara. Like most first days of school, today's topics were course orientation and classroom procedures, followed by student introductions.

Mrs. McNamara paired students and instructed the class to think of three questions they wanted to ask their partner. Anh's mind raced as she searched for the phrasing of each question, and before she could finish writing them in her notebook, her partner began.

"If you could have any superpower, what would it be?"

"What?"

"Superpower, what's your superpower?" Her partner jerked slightly forward, with a growing smirk.

"I don't know."

The interview went on like this for the next two questions. When it was Anh's turn to ask her questions, she stared at the page.

"What is your name?" Anh asked flatly.

"Michael"

"How old are you?" she continued.

"Twelve."

Before Anh could ask her third question, the shock from the sudden clanging of the bell jolted her backward.

"What is happening?" asked Anh, startled.

"Uh, class is over?" her partner offered sarcastically as he packed up his belongings and stood up.

"Where are you going?" Anh asked.

"Room 312."

"Why? When is the math teacher coming?" said Anh.

"Math teacher? The math classrooms are in hall 2."

At this point, Anh stopped asking questions because the answers made no sense. "Anh, you need to go to your next class or you'll be late," Mrs. McNamara said. Anh followed the rest of the students out the door, and down the hallway.

A few weeks into the year, Anh had internalized the rhythm of middle school, but she still had zero friends. Not being in class with the same students all day made it difficult to connect, which was compounded by her developing English skills.

Anh had reached an intermediate level of oral proficiency by the end of her US kindergarten experience, and her accent remained slight, but her earlier conversational ability had slipped over time. In her school in Vietnam, she had thirty-five minutes per week of English as a foreign language instruction, which helped, but that wasn't an adequate opportunity to use it so she wouldn't lose it.

Although Anh now understood her new routine, she continued to struggle with comprehending lessons. Every day, Mrs. McNamara started the social studies class by showing the lesson objective on her first slide, and then she asked the class what they already knew about the topic. Anh tried to pay attention, but after a minute or so of not understanding, her mind drifted to other concerns.

"Ann, honey, I need your eyes on me," Mrs. McNamara called out from the whiteboard.

Anh continued doodling in her notebook.

Mrs. McNamara walked to Anh's desk.

"Ann, pay attention."

Anh snapped back to noticing her surroundings, the way a computer wakes up when someone jiggles the mouse.

"Remember, we have to use evidence to support our positions." Mrs. McNamara told the class.

Anh looked up at the objective, *Compare power, authority, and governance in different countries' political systems.*

"You're from another country." Mrs. McNamara told Anh. "Do you think America's elections are democratic?"

Anh stayed silent.

"Be sure to state the evidence for your position."

More silence.

"Ann?"

"I don't understand."

Ms. McNamara had reached the limit of her wait time.

"OK... can someone else help Ann with the answer?"

Hands sprang up like a flare. Anh listened uncomfortably while the others stated their opinions. This time when the bell rang, Anh was packed up and ready to go.

After dinner that evening, Anh went straight to her room, shutting the door behind her. She plopped down onto her oversized beanbag chair, facing the wall above her bed. Looking back at her were the K-Pop boy band BTS, teen singer-songwriter Billie Eilish, and reggaetón artist Bad Bunny, suspended on posters ornamented with color-changing strip lights, topped by a thin metallic clothesline whose clips displayed photos of her friends and family in Vietnam.

Her bedroom door opened, and in walked Hong.

"Anh, are you doing OK?"

"Yeah, I'm OK."

Hong pursed her lips and took a deep breath.

"No, really. What's wrong?"

Anh looked up at her mother for a couple seconds, and exhaled.

"Something is wrong with this school."

"What do you mean, *something is wrong with this school*? It's a good school!" said Hong, convinced.

"School is supposed to be fun in the US. At my other school, we did so many cool things. We made stuff, we went places. At this school, all we do is work on our reading, writing, and math."

Hong bent down and sat on the floor, facing Anh.

"You like science. You wouldn't stop talking about those fossils your teacher brought to class."

Anh looked briefly at her mother's taut brow, moved her gaze to Hong's tightly grasped hands, and smiled faintly.

"Yeah, that was fun. That day I could understand most of what the teacher said, too. It's just that we don't have many days like that."

Anh told Hong that she was failing social studies, and that she was placed in a developmental reading class to boost her test scores. Hong leaned forward, mouth agape.

"You're an excellent reader! Your reading marks back home were always great. We expect you to be at the top of your class here, too. You just have to work harder."

"But, Mom . . . it's the teachers . . ." Anh took in a series of tiny inward breaths and began shaking gently. "My social studies teacher calls me Ann. She writes my name A-n-n. If Mrs. McNamara can't even get my name right, shouldn't she realize how hard learning social studies in English is for me?"

"You don't get to pick your teachers," said Hong as she wiped her index finger across Anh's wet cheek. "We've told you that many times. You have to adapt to them. It doesn't matter that you don't like her. It's your responsibility to do well, no matter who the teacher is."

Anh shook her head.

"But I don't understand her and I don't know what she wants. Today she asked me something about if I think American elections are fair. I didn't know what answer would make her happy. She kept saying, *share your honest opinion*."

The real meaning of this directive perplexed them both, and they sat together silently, pondering the right action, until Hong offered her insight.

"Well, you do have to be careful what you say, Anh. You were right not to say anything."

"I know. She kept picking on me, though."

Hong had no suggestion for Anh's last lament. It was time to put some perspective on the whole situation.

"Stay strong and work hard, Anh. You have to do well in school. To be able to give you this opportunity, our family crossed turbulent oceans on an unseaworthy raft, slowly starving for weeks."

"No, we didn't. We came on American Airlines," Anh refuted.

Hong felt a quick flush of anger, but seeing Anh's mischievous expression, she ended up laughing.

"I'm going to text some of my friends who have children in US middle schools to see what they think. Maybe together we can figure out how things work here."

Ms. Washington, Chevron's English for Speakers of Other Languages (ESOL) resource teacher, was in regular contact with Anh, checking on her progress and offering help to her teachers, never giving up on those who said they didn't need it. Of all the faculty at Chevron, Ms. Washington was Anh's favorite. She felt close enough to her to invite her to her family's temple for the Tet Lunar New Year celebration, and Ms. Washington actually showed up. Of the many invited guests in attendance, Ms. Washington was one of the few who knew to take her shoes off before entering the building. That did not go unnoticed.

Ms. Washington went to Mrs. McNamara's class the next morning and asked for Anh. Mrs. McNamara motioned to Anh to step into the hallway and shushed the students who made fun of her for being in trouble.

"I spoke with your counselor yesterday. I'm trying to get you out of the developmental reading class next term so you can choose an elective instead," said Ms. Washington empathetically.

"That's so great, thank you!"

"I said I was trying, but it isn't definite yet. You need to help."

"How?"

"I made you an appointment to meet with him this afternoon. You need to make your case why an elective would be better than the reading course. And, here, take your reading scores, and show him you're just two points away from testing out."

Ms. Washington handed Anh a folder holding her school records.

When Ms. Washington opened the classroom door for Anh, Mrs. McNamara stepped outside. "When you get a chance, I'd like to get some ideas to help Ann. When the year began, and she could barely speak English, I was pretty sure she was going to fail. But now, she's working very hard for a C, and I think that by the end of the year, she'll make it."

Ms. Washington nodded. "Of course! That's what I'm here for."

Later that day when Anh met with her counselor, he was still undecided. Anh had made a list of talking points, but she left it in her backpack and just spoke from the heart. When she was done, he looked at her test scores, nodded, and handed her a matrix with a choice of electives. "Home economics, band, computers," Anh muttered as she scanned the schedule, cheering inside. "Here's one that will fit. Art. I think that's want I want to take."

The next Monday, Anh was the first student to enter the art classroom, choosing a blue stool at a table near the shelves stocked with tempera paint bottles, a good position, she reasoned, for getting what she needed. Ms. Plein walked over to Anh, introduced herself, and held out a supplies list.

Once the classroom was full, Ms. Plein began by showing a watercolor scene that she had painted, asking students to write a few descriptive words in their notebooks. Anh's had *soft*, *colors*, and *drip*.

"During this term, we're going to start with watercolors, then we'll move to tempera," Ms. Plein said as she pointed toward Anh. "We'll also work with mixed media, and finally with digital graphics." Ms. Plein pointed to previous students' work on the walls when she mentioned each medium.

It all sounded good to Anh. She glanced at her tablemates, all boys, to see their reaction. They seemed to be into it, too. One of them, Diego, met her gaze, raising his eyebrows and tilting his head back. Anh quickly looked down and smiled knowingly, like they both were in on a secret.

"You like anime?" Diego asked.

"Sure," Anh responded, noncommittally.

Diego opened his notebook and showed her page after page of Demon Slayer manga characters. "I want to learn to draw like that."

"I don't know what I want to draw," sighed Anh.

"You'll figure it out," Diego replied.

Dinner was late because that afternoon Hong met on Zoom with the online Vietnamese Moms Group, and she had so many questions that they talked for ninety minutes. Hong put the last bowl on the table and began recounting what she had learned.

"My friends told me that American students are expected to say what they think."

Anh listened intently, then she countered that notion.

"I don't think I can do that, Mom. That goes against everything you and my teachers in Hue City taught me."

Hong started to interject but stopped herself.

Anh continued, "Even if I could make myself do it, I'd be so worried that I said something wrong."

Hong paused, then said, "Well, maybe just try something small. Don't be too honest!"

The thought of it made Anh's stomach tighten.

"My friends told me something else. They said that young people here have boyfriends and girlfriends in middle school. Is that how it is at Chevron?"

Anh thought about how cute Diego was and how flattered she was by his attention. She had imagined them being a couple, sharing their drawings with one another at the neighborhood coffee shop.

"No, no," Anh said indignantly. "No, not like that at all. It must be different here from whatever state they're from."

"Oh, good," Hong confirmed, relieved. "In our culture, we wait until we are adults. Be very careful to not let anyone get the wrong idea about you, Anh."

Anh shook her head in agreement.

The Chevron Middle School Visual and Performing Arts Festival was two weeks away. Students were rehearsing lines, warming up their voices, building sets, and adding final brushstrokes to their paintings, but Anh was stuck. She had tried to paint a watercolor of a reticulated giraffe feeding on high grass, neck bent down between its front legs, but she muddied the colors of its markings and couldn't find a way to fix it. At this point, she was running out of time, but Anh was determined to have her art displayed.

As Anh was staring at her flawed watercolor portrait, Ms. Plein walked up behind her.

"What are you thinking, Anh?"

"I want to throw this in the garbage."

"Other than the muddy colors, it's very good."

"Thanks, but I'm not going to submit something I messed up. Can I try to make something else?"

Ms. Plein showed Anh a few art books to spur ideas, and she encouraged her to select something doable given the time frame. After browsing through a couple volumes, Anh saw something that felt familiar, and she used it for inspiration as she spent every free moment of the next two weeks creating her artwork.

On the night of the festival, Anh, Hong, Tranh, and Hien walked into the packed auditorium, finding four seats together behind a column near the back. Impressed by the range of talent, Anh's family cheered after each skit, musical performance, and dance, and stood and clapped at the end with everyone else in attendance.

While the audience was still applauding, Anh motioned to her family to follow her, quickly. They maneuvered through the crowd to the library, where students' art was displayed. She saw Diego and gave a subtle waive.

Anh moved to her artwork, standing just to the right of the easel.

"Vietnam! That's Vietnam," Tranh said.

Anh smiled and nodded.

"The pagoda. We took you there when you were little!"

In front of Anh's charcoal drawing of Thien Mu Pagoda were miniature copies of the photos from her bedroom wall. She had woven her Vietnamese friends and family photographs together into the shape of a lotus flower, following the style of Vietnamese American artist Dinh Q. Lê.

Tranh touched his finger to one photo.

"You found grandma," said Anh.

The family stood there, shoulder to shoulder, transposed for a minute to where they came from.

"Anh's very talented," Ms. Plein said as she interrupted the family's sweet interlude.

They all smiled.

"And smart, too."

Anh looked to her left, where the comment came from.

"Ms. Washington!"

"Nice to see you again, Ms. Washington. This time with shoes!" joked Hong.

"Are you ready for the seventh grade, because the seventh grade is ready for you?!" said Ms. Washington.

"I am," Anh replied.

The room was filled with young artists and their families, all proud of their talents and accomplishments. Each had worked hard to adapt to middle school, but no one more than Anh.

EPILOGUE

Birth Home (or Family's Place of Origin) to US Home

Vietnam's population is close to 100 million. Modern Vietnam's economy is industrial and market based, evolving in the mid-1980s from a primarily agrarian society. About 20 percent of Vietnam's exports are sent to the US, the largest purchaser of its trades. Vietnamese is the country's official language, and 95 percent of its population is literate.[1]

Vietnam's land mass extends about a thousand miles from north to south and ranges from approximately thirty to three hundred miles from east to west. To its north is China, the South China Sea borders its east and south and the Gulf of Thailand its southwest, and Cambodia and Laos comprise its western boundary. Although the country is known for its Red and Mekong river deltas, its mountain ranges include peaks of six thousand feet and above, with the tallest, Fan Si Peak, at over ten thousand feet.

Anh's family had moved from their countryside village in the south of Vietnam to Hue City for work and educational opportunities after her Uncle Bao relocated to the US. Similar to Orlando in average monthly temperatures, Hue City has a dry season from April to August, and a rainy season from August to January. With more Buddhist monasteries than anywhere else in Vietnam, Hue City is famous for its historic buildings and monuments that line the Perfume River.

Community in the United States

After the Vietnam War, in 1975, approximately 125,000 Vietnamese refugees who had been affiliated with the US military or the South Vietnamese government were given passage to the United States for resettlement. Subsequently, in the late 1970s, another wave of Vietnamese refugees, referred to by some as "boat people," escaped from rural areas to the US and other countries, mainly Australia, Canada, and France. Current estimates of Vietnamese immigrants in the US range from 1.3 to 2 million, which is about 3 percent of the overall immigrant population. The four states with the highest numbers of Vietnamese immigrants are California, Texas, Washington State, and Florida. Sixty-six percent of Vietnamese immigrants currently living in the US entered the country before 2000, with 18 percent arriving between 2000 and 2009, and 16 percent in 2010 or after. Recent figures indicate that 97 percent of Vietnamese immigrants who become US permanent residents do so through family reunification, which is well above the 68 percent of all recent permanent residents who gain their residency status through this program. Many Vietnamese immigrants provide financial support to their families in Southeast Asia, with recent annual remittances equaling $14 billion, approximately 6 percent of the country's GDP.[2]

As a group, Vietnamese immigrants come to the US with less education than other Asians, with 21 percent of Vietnamese emigrating with a bachelor's degree, in comparison to 30 percent of all Asians. The age of first-generation Vietnamese immigrants also diverges from overall Asian averages. The median age of foreign-born Vietnamese is five years older than that of all foreign-born Asians in the US. Median annual household income for US Vietnamese is $60,000, compared to all US Asians' median income of $73,060.[3] There is tremendous variation among groups classified as Asians, so it is especially important to know the basic history and facts about English learners' specific home countries. For information on different Asian groups in the US, a good resource is the Pew Research Center Asian Americans webpage, which includes fact sheets on Asians from different national origins.[4]

From 2000 to 2015, the US Asian population grew faster than any other ethnicity or race, with the majority of Asian Americans being of Chinese, Indian, and Filipino origin. Americans whose families originated in Vietnam and Korea round out the top five nations that Asians emigrated from. These figures reflect not only first-generation immigrants from Asia but also second generation and beyond who identify as Asian American.[5] There is a general misconception that all Asian students are high achieving, coming from families that are "model minorities." While this might seem like a beneficial public impression of Asian students, these types of generalizations are detrimental, creating unfounded expectations based on race.[6]

US citizens can petition for close family members to obtain a green card or a nonimmigrant visa. As a naturalized US citizen, Bao was eligible to petition for green cards for his brother, Tranh, and Tranh's wife, Hong, and their application was approved because Bao's real estate company had a strong financial track record and pledged a living wage to each. There are a number of visa options related to working in the United States, from H-1B temporary, nonimmigrant, worker visas to EB-5 immigrant investor visas for establishing a business in the US.[7]

Anh's mother, Hong, sought advice and encouragement from an online network of immigrant moms who live in the US, a trend that moms from many different countries participate in. Social media enable connections that help immigrant families navigate the struggles of adapting to a new culture and language while maintaining what they hold dear from their home cultures and languages. As noted in Anh's story, a common concern among Vietnamese parents of children in US secondary schools is peer pressure to develop physical or amorous relationships with other students, which occurs at a younger age than the norm in Vietnamese culture.

School

Middle school is a critical time in any student's education, but for English learners, this period is especially significant. Research from Florida middle schools shows that students transitioning to middle school are at risk of obtaining substantially lower test scores than in earlier grades and of feeling socially unsafe.[8] After six consecutive years of sharing the same teacher and room with their class, students entering middle school experience the unsettledness of learning subjects with different teachers and moving to different classrooms, which makes developing relationships with teachers and classmates more difficult. The US middle school concept and structure differ from the educational system in Vietnam, where even into secondary school, teachers come to the students' classroom, avoiding the boisterous movement of students in the halls from period to period that characterizes American secondary school. According to the Center for Responsive Schools, children at the age of twelve, Anh's age, are primarily concerned with seeking approval from their peers to establish their identity.[9] Programs that emphasize social-emotional learning can help middle school students feel that they belong socially and academically, which, in turn, has been shown to improve their psychological health and course grades.[10] Chevron Middle has been piloting a program that infuses social-emotional learning into multiple courses in all grades.

Another challenging aspect of middle school for English learners is the rising language demands. In *Educating English Learners*, my coauthors and I discuss how the complexity of language used in classroom instruction and assessment rises with each grade level, putting English learners who enter upper grades as newcomers at a disadvantage.[11] With state standards that increase in rigor comes language that increases in complexity, and EL students have double the work in learning the challenging content *through* English while they are learning to listen, speak, read, and write *in* English. National Assessment of Educational Progress (NAEP) achievement levels from 2019 illustrate this point. In fourth grade, 10 percent of EL students are at or above proficient in reading, but in eighth grade, only 4 percent are (the percent of non-ELs at or above proficient is 39 in fourth grade and 36 in eighth).[12] This is not entirely due to newcomers at beginning levels of proficiency entering middle school, as some English learners who entered US schools as early as kindergarten may continue to struggle to reach grade-level proficiency into the middle school years. English learners who began schooling in the US in kindergarten and are not reclassified as non-English learners by the fifth grade are commonly referred to as long-term English learners, a matter of increasing concern nationally.[13]

Due to unwavering emphases on standardized testing in public schools, some secondary schools have replaced English-learner-specific English Language Development/ESOL classes with general reading development classes. Although it might seem appropriate to group EL students with non-EL students who also need to improve their reading, English learners, especially those who are still developing oral proficiency, need specialized instruction that takes the processes of second language acquisition into account.[14] In Anh's case, the reading course was not appropriate to her needs and filled time in her schedule that could have been used for an elective. Many English learners at the secondary level are unable to participate in electives because of reading development or other courses that support the development of English proficiency, and it is important to find opportunities for them to explore areas such as the arts, where undiscovered talents could be developed. For Anh, visual arts provided an outlet for expressing her identity as a Vietnamese American and for developing a sense of self-efficacy in a subject that didn't depend on her English proficiency to excel in.

Mrs. McNamara played a key role in Anh's struggle to adjust to school in the US. Although she was not knowledgeable about how to support Anh's learning, she eventually did reach out to Ms. Washington to ask for guidance. Ms. Washington helped her with providing more English-learner friendly ways to communicate social studies concepts, such as the show tools and techniques in our book *Show, Tell, Build*.[15] Ms. Washington also discussed how she might approach an upcoming chapter on the Vietnamese War, acknowledging the valuable, potentially contrasting perspective Anh and her family could provide but without putting her on the spot or emphasizing her otherness. One issue that Ms. Washington highlighted was the importance of knowing and validating her students' names, especially when they are uncommon. She introduced her to the My Name, My Identity: A Declaration of Self project, which prompted Mrs. McNamara to pledge to pronounce her students' names correctly.[16] Ms. Washington helped her develop a mnemonic device to remember (Anh is always on!).

Family

Because members of Anh's extended family had made Orlando their new home, Tranh, Hong, Anh, and Hien had the mooring of family ties as they grew accustomed to their new lives in the US. This gave them many affordances that other immigrant families lack. In addition, residing within a Vietnamese expatriate community concentrated along Colonial Drive (the irony of its name lost on most of Orlando's residents) fostered a sense of belonging and built the many shared resources of social capital. This provided benefits for Anh's family, but because the community had been established decades earlier, Anh had no Vietnamese English-learner peers in her classes.

Even though Anh's nuclear family did not personally experience the tribulations of being refugees, their extended family's struggles were a big part of their family lore. Hong spoke with her moms' group about how they use their families' immigration stories to motivate their children to succeed, a near universal experience among them. They told their children often about the sacrifices and difficulties their relatives made so that they would have opportunities to live productive, meaningful lives, building a deep sense of responsibility to succeed, which honors the selflessness of their family members and ancestors.

Student

Anh's experience personifies a number of English-learner characteristics and typical situations they face, many of which reflect the experiences of students from very different backgrounds. For instance, English learners from different countries start school in the US for different reasons, and some return home for an interval of varying length, with a portion of those students eventually moving back to the US. This coming and going has benefits and drawbacks for the students' achievement in US schools. In Anh's case, having spent her kindergarten year in the US enabled her to acquire a measure of oral proficiency and literacy in English, a definite benefit for learning her second language. She also had yearly instruction in English while she was in school in Vietnam, but the classes lasted only thirty-five minutes per week, so there was a substantial loss of proficiency over time. However, the foundation she built at an early age was partially retrievable when she reentered school in the US, which gave her a distinct advantage over newcomers at Chevron who arrived without any prior knowledge of English. Moving from one school system and language of instruction to another repeatedly presents numerous challenges, including some of the effects of interrupted education such as gaps in knowledge, even if the student was continuously enrolled in school during the periods of upheaval.

Anh was reticent about speaking in class and about giving her opinion in particular. There could be many reasons for her reluctance to speak, including self-consciousness about her developing English proficiency and her somewhat shy personality in any situation. The conversation she had with Hong shows that something else was going on, something with cultural dimensions. In her schooling experiences in Vietnam, students typically didn't speak in class. The teacher did. Moreover, it was uncommon for teachers to solicit students' opinions, whether they were based on evidence or not. Vietnamese students put in these situations in the US can feel very anxious about expressing their thoughts, especially in controversial or critical situations. In Anh's experience with her social studies class, when she did muster the courage to speak her mind, she worried for weeks afterward if she had angered or hurt her teacher or classmates unintentionally with her answer.

Anh finished the sixth grade barely passing some core subjects, but a pass is a pass. She excelled in her art course and ended up with a B in science and math. By the end of the year, she had earned a B on her social studies final exam, which brought her course grade up to a C. Her progress and success encouraged her to continue to work hard to reach even higher levels of achievement.

ANH'S STORY DISCUSSION QUESTIONS

1. Anh's parents emphasized their family's immigration story to motivate Anh and Hien to work hard in school. EL students sometimes feel pressure to be worthy of the sacrifices their families made. Do you think this is more of a burden or an inspiration?
2. Anh had spent time in a US school at a much earlier age and then returned permanently years after. What are the benefits and drawbacks of

staying at the same school for any student (EL or otherwise)? How might moving from school to school in different countries complicate an EL student's educational experience? How might it give them an advantage?

3. Anh was reluctant to answer questions in class. A number of factors could be at play. Why do you think she was so reticent, and how might Mrs. McNamara have helped her participate more?
4. How did Anh's earlier memories of being in the US affect her adaptation to living here now?
5. Anh was placed in a developmental reading course because of her test scores. Do you think that was the best way to help her improve her English skills? What other ways could be effective?
6. Anh's mother, Hong, connected online with other Vietnamese moms. How could Anh's teachers have advised Hong to use this resource to support Anh's success? What questions or requests would you suggest that a parent of an EL student post to these types of support groups?
7. How did having the opportunity to take an art elective affect Anh's attitude and confidence?

CHAPTER 5

DANI'S STORY

TEN YEARS' STUDY of direct and indirect objects, past participles, and irregular plurals didn't prepare Dani well for hallway conversations at Alcove High School, deep in the heart of Texas. The overcrowded corridors reverberated with full-bodied greetings, the kind expressed after months apart, but "How do you do?," the textbook English salutation Dani learned back home in northern Iraq, was not heard among them. Hearing anything recognizable was a struggle.

Walking with a printed schedule of his classes, Dani scanned the placards next to each door. E17, E15, E12. First period, Developmental Math, was in E13. He looked at both sides of the hallway. He walked down to the end. No E13.

"Aaah, mmm, E 13?," Dani asked a boy nearby.

"E30? That's in another building."

Dani looked puzzled.

"That way," the boy indicated, pointing somewhere distant, and to the right.

Dani's family roots reach centuries deep in the rugged region northeast of the Tigris River, near a small village called Hiror, where Toyota and Peugeot sedans share the road with livestock. His ancestors built their homestead on fifteen acres, an ideal site for growing fig trees and raising sheep. The original home, which still stands, was made of rough stones cemented together with mustard-colored mortar, topped by a thatched roof made of twigs. Their new house, built in the 1970s, was also a basic square layout with a flat-pitched roof, but its walls were made of cinder blocks and its roof concrete. Surrounding their home was forbiddingly mountainous terrain, punctured by land mines buried beneath the rocky surface. Freezing in the winter and blisteringly hot in the summer, Hiror's landscape features gushing waterfalls and white-capped river rapids. It is a beautiful and perilous place.

Because of its remote location, Hiror is quite cut off from the world, with very limited internet access in town or its surroundings. While the young people in the big cities like Erbil watched YouTube videos and communicated by Skype, Dani had scant experience with these technologies, and he spent most of his time playing ball or studying.

After working as an engineer, helping to rebuild roads and bridges in his war-torn homeland, Dani's father, Rebin, applied for a US State Department scholarship to study in the US. Fifteen years earlier, Rebin had completed his undergraduate studies in civil engineering at the University of Dohuk, and since then, Rebin and his wife, Azade, consistently put away $500 a year for graduate school. The time was right, they thought, for Rebin to pursue a master's degree at the University of Texas, Tyler, a designated institution for scholarship awardees.

As Rebin and Azade planned for the study-abroad experience, they had many important decisions to make. Dani's brother had just turned nineteen and was admitted to the University of Dohuk, so everyone agreed that Dani, who was entering the eleventh grade, and his sister, Sevîn, a rising fifth grader, would join Rebin and Azade for this American adventure.

"This is it, right? 47 Doval Avenue."

Rebin checked his paper.

"Yes, this is the place," he said.

"That'll be $35," the taxi driver said while pointing to the meter.

Rebin pulled a $20, a $10, and a $5 out of his wallet, bulging with cash from the airport exchange, and handed it to the cab driver.

The cabbie yanked the trunk release.

"Get your bags back there," he said as he scrolled his phone.

"OK," Rebin said, motioning to Dani to help.

Dani lifted the heaviest bag out and commented to his father in Arabic. "So far, Dad, Americans haven't been very friendly."

"I know! This guy seemed nice at first, but by the time we got here, he was downright angry."

"Yeah. Maybe the traffic stressed him out," Dani surmised.

"Right! I've never seen such wide streets!"

The Nebez family's new home was an apartment in an outdated complex affiliated with student housing. There were three bedrooms and one bath, a setup intended for roommates in sets of three. The walls had been patched and painted white, the carpet had been shampooed, and the unit was completely empty. It was too late to go anywhere, so they spent their first night sleeping on the floor.

In the morning, the whole family walked to Walmart, which was only three blocks away. As the cars sped by on the six-lane road, they realized they would have to cross the street at the next intersection. Rebin saw the cars coming to a stop when the light turned red, so he promptly stepped off the curb. A loud skidding sound ensued, causing Rebin to jump back onto the sidewalk reflexively. Stunned, he stared at the pickup truck as it slowly resumed its right turn, while Dani and Sevîn, in Azade's tight and trembling grip, stood still as statues.[1]

After waiting through a few lights, they finally made it to the superstore, purchasing some groceries they recognized and forgoing any furniture and other necessities for their apartment. Safely back at home, they were putting the perishables in the refrigerator when the landlord knocked on the door to finalize the move-in paperwork. Noting that the apartment was bare, she took them to a storage room with furniture and plates, pots, pans, and even decorations that previous occupants had left behind. They were able to get almost everything they needed for free, and the rest they purchased at a nearby thrift shop.

Rebin had expected to get acclimated to US graduate-level English requirements by enrolling in UT Tyler's upper-level ESL classes for a month or so, but his first visit to campus included a three-hour English proficiency exam, after which an adviser told him he was 32 points from meeting the minimum score of 79. This difference required him to spend far more time than expected at the university's intensive English program, where he was placed in the low intermediate level. It was an unanticipated setback, as the family was confident of Rebin's English skills after many years of dedicated independent study. Now, it would take almost a year for him to enter the master's in engineering program. Fortunately, his scholarship covered the additional expenses. Azade was grateful for the extended financial support, but she worried about how the additional year would affect the children's education. She kept that concern to herself, though, not wanting to add to Rebin's disappointment.

On the Thursday before school began, the entire family took the city bus to deliver Dani's school records to Alcove High. Dani's translated report cards listed Mathematics 1, 2, and 3, which had no equivalent in Alcove's course codes, so the school counselor arranged for a math and reading placement test. The results put Dani in developmental courses for both subjects, with Intensive Science,

English 1, Physical Education, Computer Literacy, and American History rounding out his schedule.

The next day, Rebin used his new Tracfone to look up the address of the closest mosque and to call for an Uber. The trip there was short and silent. As the car neared the building, Rebin was able to make out a familiar form in the distance. He began to smile as if he had run into an old friend. "Look there! I see something you'll recognize." Sevîn peered in between the front headrests and locked focus on the dome that topped the building. "There it is!" she exclaimed. The closer the car came to its destination, the louder a lilting call rang, sung with sustained, piercing tones punctuated by rapidly ascending and descending notes, no rhythm, no melody, no instruments, just the solitary human voice. Five times a day Dani had heard this sound, for all of his life until this week. Hearing it today evoked feelings of peacefulness and serenity, a near instant reconnection.

Standing in front of the complex, the family felt a sense of belonging, a bond signaled by sight and sound.

"Look!" Sevîn gestured toward a rusty 1957 Ford flatbed with Texas plates, parked under a nearby pecan tree.

Azade smiled and hugged her. "Maybe we need one of those Texas cars so we can drive to the mosque," Azade suggested. "It looks like fun."

"It's about time you got here," said Dani's math teacher, Mr. Parker. "You must be Dana."

"Dah-nee" Dani said matter-of-factly.

"There's a desk back there. You'll need to see me after class, OK?"

Dani nodded, unsure of what he was agreeing to.

Dani sat down and opened his notebook. He watched intently as Mr. Parker's right arm cast a thick shadow across the interactive whiteboard, drawing attention to a projected equation, $2x + 2 = 6$. Dani squinted to see the numbers. He had solved these kinds of problems years ago. Was high school math in America this easy?

"Now, explain to me how y'all made sense of this problem. Show me your mathematical reasonin,'" Mr. Parker said while looking for raised hands.

Yes, his teacher spoke slowly, but those sentences came at Dani fast, much faster than for others in the class. The words were nothing but scattered sounds running into one another— "*naueksplentumihauyalmedsensuvthIsprablum . . .*" That's what came through to Dani.

After class, Mr. Parker summoned Dani as he headed toward the door. Dani walked up to the front, standing face-to-face with his teacher. Mr. Parker inched backward, looked at Dani for a second and began, "I don't tolerate tardiness, Dani. You're a junior—you should know better."

Dani stood there, expressionless, at full attention.

Mr. Parker took a step back. Dani moved closer.

Mr. Parker reached his right arm forward, palm toward Dani.

"Move back."

Dani looked around. "I no understand."

"¡Muévete!" Mr. Parker exclaimed.

"I beg pardon?" offered Dani.

Mr. Parker flicked his hand upward, to the right.

"You're dismissed. Sal de aquí."

During his planning period, Mr. Parker walked to the counseling offices. He found Dani's assigned adviser, Mr. Álvarez, and asked if he had a minute.

"This kid, Dani Rebez, came late to my class today. I asked to speak with him after, but he didn't seem to understand English. So, I used my Spanish 101 with him, and he got right up in my face. Why isn't he in a bilingual class?"

Mr. Álvarez opened Dani's folder.

"The student doesn't speak Spanish. He's from Iran."

The counselor flipped through Dani's papers.

"Or maybe Iraq. One or the other. In any case, he doesn't speak Spanish."

"But his name sounds Spanish," Mr. Parker said, yet unconvinced.

"You'll need to learn Arabic if you want to talk to him in his language!" Mr. Álvarez said, laughing.

Later that evening Dani told Rebin and Azade about his tough day, how he couldn't find his classroom and got in trouble in first period. He described Mr. Parker's strange way of speaking, almost incomprehensible, with weird words like "yawl," which, Dani explained, is some kind of sailboat, because he looked it up. Mr. Parker was so hard to understand that at some point, it seemed he was speaking another language altogether.

"Dani, you're strong. You overcome challenges with humor. Since you were little, your teachers told me you make your class laugh. You can do that here, too, once you learn to speak like they do," Azade reminded him.

"Sure, Mom," Dani offered, wondering if it was too late to change his mind about leaving Iraq.

A few weeks into the fall semester, Mr. Parker noticed that whenever he gave the class numeric equations, Dani solved them first and best. But Dani never explained how he got his answers, and he also left word problems blank on quizzes and tests. Something was there, but the most important things were missing. Trying to understand what was going on with Dani, Mr. Parker caught up with a bilingual education teacher who taught math.

> "I've got an Arabic student who's struggling in my class. He seems to be trying, but how can I help if I don't know the kid's language?"
>
> "Can he speak any English?" asked the bilingual teacher.
>
> "A little, but he can't explain anything he does. You know that's required to pass tests now, so it's a real concern. All he can do is hold a simple conversation in broken English."
>
> "Well, that's a start. You have something to work with."

The bilingual teacher shared some tools and techniques that worked for his students. Mr. Parker tried a couple that week and saw a difference almost immediately. Dani participated, explaining his answers by filling in the blanks, as in "*My solution is________. I arrived at my solution by________,*" with terms he selected from a word list that included "dividing, multiplying" and so on. Encouraged by the effect of his new approach, that weekend Mr. Parker drove to a local bookstore and bought an English/Arabic dictionary, hoping to help Dani translate math terms he had learned back home.

About a month later, when Mr. Parker's students were working in groups, one of the boys asked Dani if he was going to the Longhorns' semifinals on Friday.

> "The football match?" Dani inquired.
>
> "It's a football *game*, not match. Matches are for chess," another boy responded.
>
> "I play football in Hiror," Dani pointed out.

"Were you on your school team?"

"My school have no team. I play in my city."

"So, are you coming? We're all going to be there."

Being asked to join the boys was the first time anyone included Dani since he arrived at Alcove High.

"Thank you for ask me," Dani said softly. "I busy all Fridays. Pardon."

Everyone was back from winter break, and for Dani, it felt like a fresh start. After passing Developmental Math, Dani made a successful case to skip Algebra 1 and enroll in Geometry. Dani had passed all courses, barely, with the exception of English 1, which frustrated him because he clearly knew English grammar rules better than anyone else. One time, he was the only student who realized that "between you and me" was actually correct because "me" was the object of the preposition. That didn't stop Dani from having to repeat the course, though.

This semester the class Dani was most excited about was biology. Ms. Mudaris was a first-year teacher, fresh out of college, filled with the latest instructional knowledge and skills as well as the boundless enthusiasm a first real job inspires. Before the new term, Ms. Mudaris had meticulously designed seating charts based on student files, which she pored over at the end of every December school day.

Knowing she had two students from the same country, Ms. Mudaris put Dani's desk next to Nawras, a new student from Basra. When class began, she asked the class members to introduce themselves, starting with Nawras.

"My name is Nawras. I am Iraqi."

Ms. Mudaris grinned.

Next was Dani.

"I am Dani. I am Kurdish, from Hiror."

Nawras spun his head toward Dani and scoffed.

Dani continued, unaware, smiling at his new classmates.

Nearly the entire class period was taken up by the introductions, and when class ended, Nawras looked over to Dani, pulled on his jacket sleeve, and addressed him in Arabic.

"Why'd you say you're Kurdish? You're from Iraq!"

Dani's neck stiffened.

"That's where I'm from."

"You are Iraqi! You should say it proudly."

Ms. Mudaris walked over to the boys.

"I can see you two have a lot in common. It's great to see you talking together in your language! Nawras, you're lucky that Dani is in class with you. He's been here a semester, and he can help you understand everything."

They both nodded slightly, without expression, then Nawras stood up to leave.

Despite the situation with Nawras, Dani still liked his biology class the most, because of Ms. Mudaris, of course, but also because a group of boys that sat near him were in the robotics club and told Dani how much fun it was, also letting him know that Ms. Mudaris was the club sponsor. Dani attended the next meeting, where the array of cutting-edge technology dazzled him, and the assemblage of science-loving students welcomed him as if he had always been one of them.

While tinkering with motors and gears, one of the boys asked Dani about his family.

"How many brothers and sisters do you have, Dani? Are they all here?"

"I have little sister. She in elementary school here. I also have big brother, but he study at Dohuk University."

"You must miss him," said the boy, while the others looked on.

"Yes, my brother want come visit last month, but he was in hospital, from drinking milk."

"Oh, I'm sorry. Did he get food poisoning?" the boy asked.

"No, the cow fall on him," Dani deadpanned.

Dani's teammates looked at each other, completely silent. Could that be normal in Iraq? They turned toward Dani, who stayed stone-faced for at least five beats. Just before anyone could ask a question or register a complaint, Dani yelled, "I am joking! He is OK. He have no money for plane ticket."

"Was it a longhorn cow, Dani?" one of the quickest-witted boys asked, while the rest of them finally got the joke.

Rebin was working his way up to the highest level at the English institute, and earning top grades kept him exceedingly busy. After school, Azade had more time for Dani and Sevîn, and they often recapped their day before having dinner.

Azade's days were stable and routine, very different from her life as a nurse in Iraq. Here she cooked breakfast, lunch, and dinner and kept the apartment pristine. The afternoon talks with her children were the highlight of her day. Today, however, Sevîn looked distressed.

"What's wrong, Sevîn?" Azade inquired.

"The lunch lady yelled at me today," Sevîn disclosed, head bowed as she spoke.

"What for?" Azade asked, shocked.

"I couldn't understand what she was saying. I really don't know why."

Azade looked at Dani for guidance.

"Mom, let's go together to talk with Sevîn's teacher tomorrow," Dani implored.

The next afternoon, Azade, Sevîn, and Dani walked into the fifth-grade classroom, filled with groups of huddled desks and chairs, posters with helpful phrases, comfy spaces to sit and read, and bins with handy resources. They sat at one of the desk quartets, pairs facing one another. Azade started by thanking Sevîn's teacher for meeting with them; then she paused so Dani could interpret.

Dani asked Sevîn, in English, to say what happened, while the teacher looked on, concerned. Sevîn responded in Arabic, almost inaudibly, while Dani struggled to keep up with translating. Once she understood the reason for their visit, the teacher suggested they head to the kitchen to speak with the cafeteria worker, so they followed her to the lunchroom.

"Hi . . . ," said the teacher. "Yesterday you spoke with Sevîn after lunch. Was there a problem?"

"Yes, I told the girl it's wrong to throw out food. She always picks at her plate, eating the bread or fruit, and she leaves the rest."

Dani interjected. "Some foods she cannot eat."

"I don't see any allergies listed for her," said the cafeteria worker, looking at a clipboard.

"Not allergies," Dani responded.

"Well, then, is she vegetarian?"

Dani searched for words to explain his family's Halal dietary restrictions. After hesitating a moment, he simply responded, "Yes."

"Oh, I didn't know. We can serve her vegetarian meals from now on."

"Great!" said Dani. "Problem solved! Thank you for understanding."

And with that, they all smiled, stood up, and left.

Since they had arrived in Tyler, the whole family spent Sunday afternoons at the mosque, where Dani played soccer with the youth group. It hadn't taken long for the team to recognize Dani's talents, and soon he became the most consistent scorer, popularly known as "The Striker."

This Sunday, there was a new player on the field.

"Hey, Nawras! You play football, too?" Dani asked.

"Yes," Nawras replied, and tapped the ball to Dani.

"Dani's our best player," a fullback boasted.

Nawras tipped his head back and pursed his lips.

"Let's see what he can do," Nawras intoned, passing the ball back to him.

The game started, and Dani controlled the ball for most of the ninety minutes, scoring two goals. Nawras congratulated Dani for the win, the first time they talked since the beginning of the semester.

"Are you coming to the other matches this week," Dani asked.

"What about school?" Nawras responded.

"It's spring break. We have the whole week off."

"Then, yes. I'll be here tomorrow."

"Good," said Dani. "See you then."

It seemed that spring break was a line of demarcation for Dani, because now he felt he was beginning to fit in. He knew how things worked, generally, at Alcove High, and his personality had managed to break through the English barrier. Like Sevîn, Dani navigated the school cafeteria ritual by eating vegetarian meals, and he even had a group of students that he sat with, his unofficial induction into American school culture.

"Hey, Dani!" some of the boys from biology class called from back of the lunchroom.

Dani gave a *'sup* nod and carried his tray over to them.

"Read this sentence," Dani's classmate commanded, handing Dani a paper while the small group looked on.

Everyone listened to Dani, reading *Mr. Parker has perfect pitch* as "Mr. Barker has berfect bitch."

Dani looked up from his paper as the laughter got louder. He began to feel a heaviness above his chest, right where the breathy consonants of Arabic articulate. He remembered Mr. Parker's curt response to his first attempt to answer a question, in front of the entire class—"I can't understand a word you're saying, Dani!"—and how everyone started laughing at his heavy accent. Now his new friends from biology class were laughing at him, too.

Just before the ruckus stopped, Dani tipped his chin upward and started laughing along. His participation rekindled, and somehow humanized, their amusement.

"Dani, you are *so* funny!" one of the kids yelled. "You're the best!"

"Everyone tells me I should be a comedian," Dani replied. "Listen, I have some funny words to teach you in Arabic," he said with a smile.

"Yeah, teach us the bad words!" said the boy with the paper.

The dogwood was in full bloom early this spring, brightening the woods behind the track field. Banners were everywhere, cheering on the Longhorns soccer team, which placed in the state quarterfinals for the first time. Games were scheduled for the next two Thursdays, so Dani got a ride with one of his robotics team members who was a midfielder.

Curious about the differences between football in Iraq and soccer in the US, Dani sat alone in the bleachers and paid close attention to every part of the game. When it was over, he met his friend outside the locker room.

"What'd you think about the game, Dani?" his friend asked while taking off his cleats.

"Y'all played well. Too bad you couldn't win," said Dani with a grin.

"Our forward took a lot of shots, but no goals."

"Yeah, two or three times tonight I thought, *Put me in, coach! I can score!*"

"I wish he had—we might have won! Why don't you try out for next year's team, Dani? We need a center forward. It couldn't hurt to try."

Dani imagined himself out on the field, bending the ball inside the left goalpost as the chants get louder—Dani, Dani! Whether he made the team or not, he knew next year was surely going to be different.

The seniors were being fitted for their caps and gowns, and the rest of the student body waited out the last week of the year playing games in class, relieved and relaxed without the pressure of tests. The mottled gray backgrounds of junior yearbook photos were being signed in the hallways, and most comments referred to plans for next year, the great senior year of high school that all students expected to reach. Except Dani. Because he began in eleventh grade with only basic English proficiency, he would not earn enough credits to graduate on time.

Dani made an appointment with Mr. Álvarez to look at his earned credits and graduation requirements. Everyone wants to graduate with their class, and Dani was no different, but he knew that was an unattainable goal.

"Hola, Señor Álvarez," Dani greeted his counselor.

"You've learned some Spanish, too? I thought you had your hands full learning English!"

"I picked up a little Spanish from my friends on the robotics team because, you know, I want to impress you."

"I was already impressed."

Mr. Álvarez turned his monitor around so they both could see how many credits Dani earned and how many he still needed.

"I guess I can't graduate next year, right?"

"No, if everything goes well, you'll need an extra year and a half."

Dani sunk down in his chair.

"I've worked really hard. I studied twice as much as back home, and I earned half the credits."

"Don't get discouraged, Dani. There's no hurry. You just keep taking classes until you finish."

That night, Dani told Rebin and Azade about his meeting with Mr. Álvarez, letting them know how discouraged he was. Rebin, as analytical types tend to do, grabbed a notebook and pencil and made a list of Dani's options:

1. Stay in Tyler, spend an extra school year and two summers earning graduation credits.
2. Return home, repeat your grade.

Dani looked on as Rebin wrote and reached out for the paper when his father set the pencil down. He read it silently, taking about ten extra seconds before looking up.

"There's another option, Dad. Just quit."

"I'm going to pretend you didn't say that," Rebin said incredulously.

"I also need to pass five exams. I think I'll do OK with Algebra and Biology, but it'll be hard to pass two English and one US History tests."

Rebin didn't flinch.

Dani continued. "Mr. Álvarez said students still learning English, like me, have the highest dropout rate. I can see why. This was just supposed to be a one-year experience, then it became two, and now three."

"Dani, your father and I were just discussing how three years might be best for everyone. There's a yearlong internship opportunity after he finishes his master's. And who knows where we'll go after that?" Azade said with a faintly hopeful smile. Rebin nodded.

Dani returned Azade's optimistic expression, reflecting on how much he loved science and technology, and more recently, once again, math. He really did appreciate counselors and teachers who went above and beyond, the up-to-date technology and materials in his classes, and all the affordances of his big, new school, with a football stadium and a track and field. He envisioned himself right there, with the Longhorns soccer team, making MVP. His mind raced forward, past graduation, on to college. Could he study engineering at UT Tyler, like his dad? Maybe this temporary adventure would turn out to be something more permanent. Maybe home could mean more than one place.

EPILOGUE

Birth Home (or Family's Place of Origin) to US Home

The majority of Iraq's territory comprises deserts, with mountainous areas in northern regions bordering Iran and Turkey. Iraq's area is 438,317 square kilometers, roughly three times the size of New York state. Of that area, 437,367 square kilometers are land, with only 950 square kilometers of water. The country shares borders with Turkey, Iran, Kuwait, Saudi Arabia, Jordan, and Syria and is landlocked except for a small coastal area south of Basra, on the Persian Gulf. Iraq's government is a federal parliamentary republic, and its population is 38.9 million. About 70 percent of the population lives in urban areas, and the literacy rate is 50 percent. Iraq's largest export partners are India, China, and the US, and their imports come mainly from Turkey and China.[2]

The educational system in Iraq is directed by the national Iraqi Ministry of Education. Beginning at the middle school level, genders are separated.[3]

As Nawras noted, Dani is an Iraqi citizen, but his people, the Kurds, are an ethnic minority that represents about 16 percent of the Iraqi population. Iraqi Kurds are predominantly Sunni Muslim, while the majority of Iraqis are Shia Muslims.[4] Both Islamic groups share central beliefs and practices, but differences related to authority and interpretation have formed separate branches over time.[5] The Kurdish people live in southeastern Turkey, northeastern Syria, northern Iraq, northwestern Iran, and southwestern Armenia and are the world's largest group without a nation of their own.[6]

As was shown in Dani's story, it's important to find out what ethnic/language group EL students come from rather than assume that they are part of the majority in their home country. The reason these families left could be because they were persecuted by the majority, especially in cases of refugees (see Dibenesha's story for information about refugees) and asylees (see Rafael's story for information about asylees).

Community in the United States

The US Department of State uses many forms of diplomacy to create goodwill in areas of conflict. One of them is funding deserving individuals to study in the United States. Universities in the US cooperate with US government programs that support international students from these targeted regions, but because the scholarship programs select a very small number of the top applicants in each country, it's less likely that participating universities will have an established community of students from the same place. There are, however, a sizable number of Middle Eastern students in US universities, the majority of whom are either self-funded or receive scholarships from their own governments, but their countries, cultures, and languages or dialects are diverse.

In the 2019–2020 academic year, US universities hosted over 1 million international students total, which is about 5 percent of overall university enrollment. Of those, students from China and India make up over 50 percent, with students from Middle Eastern countries including Saudi Arabia at 3 percent, Iran and Turkey at 1 percent, and Kuwait and Pakistan at slightly less than 1 percent.[7] While most of these students return home, some remain in the US after completing their studies. Some of these international student immigrants become undocumented by overstaying their student visas. Others find jobs in the US after graduation, primarily in specialized fields, and their employers petition for a work permit, which allows them to eventually apply for permanent residency. And some fall in love during their stay in the US and end up marrying a US citizen, which can also lead to permanent residency.

The US has the third highest number of Middle Eastern/North African (MENA) immigrants in the world, over 1 million residents in total. Turkey's MENA immigrant population is second, with 1.6 million, and France is first, with 2.9 million. Within the US, five states are the home of over half of MENA immigrants—California (20 percent), Michigan (10 percent), New York (9 percent), and Texas and New Jersey (6 percent each). Iraqi immigrants are less likely to be proficient in English than some other MENA nationalities, such as the United Arab Emirates. Median MENA immigrant family income in the US is $45,000, $9,000 less than the median for all immigrant nationalities.[8]

School

English learners in high school face daunting challenges. The language demands of standards-based education are heavy, and learning English, the language of instruction, while learning rigorous secondary-level academic content, can lead to failure that has lifelong implications.

English learners who enter US schools for the first time in high school have the most difficulty graduating within four years, along with so-called *long-term English learners*, students classified as ELs for six years or more. In the state of Arizona, for example, long-term English learners at the high school level have a graduation rate of 49 percent versus the non–EL graduation rate of 85 percent.[9] English learners who enter US schools for the first time at the high school level, and who may have had limited or interrupted formal education (known as students with limited or interrupted formal education, or SLIFE), often due to civil unrest, war, crime, poverty, and other social issues, have the greatest challenges in graduating from high school. Dani was fortunate that Texas has an extended policy for completion of high school. Many states set age limits of twenty-one to complete high school courses, but Texas allows up to the age of twenty-six.

Dani was Alcove High School's first Iraqi student and one of the first Middle Eastern students to enroll there. Because Texas has maintained strong bilingual education programs over the last few decades, Alcove had a number of bilingual teachers who know how to teach second languages and how to teach academic subjects in students' home and second languages. As the story indicated, the school had no Arabic-speaking bilingual teachers, but some of the bilingual educators shared tips on working with students who are learning English as a second language.

Math and science had been Dani's strongest subjects in Iraq. However, the placement test at Alcove High included word problems, which required comprehension of language to solve, and although some test items were purely numeric, they used symbols Dani was unaccustomed to. For example, Dani was confused by a symbol used in the US for long division equations, the long division bracket, consisting of a short vertical line to the right of the divisor (in this case 50), connected to the long horizontal line above the dividend (in this case 2500), the vertical and horizontal lines perpendicular to one another and forming the left and top side of a rectangle, above which the quotient is written. This differs from the symbol for division that Dani had learned in Iraq (2500/50), which caused very basic errors that did not reflect Dani's depth of knowledge (Dani multiplied 50 times the square root of 2500 because he thought the bracket enclosing 2500 was an American version of the square root symbol).

Word problems are an obvious area of math where language matters tremendously. Some problems are especially wordy, including unnecessary adjectives and other superfluous language, and they may also use terms that are less common, such as "marbles." English learners can get caught up by not knowing the meaning of marbles, even if they are simply used to represent items that can be counted. When it comes to being precise, as math requires, knowing every word in a problem seems necessary. When Dani stated the word *y'all* as he heard Mr. Parker say it, his translation app identified the word *yawl* and translated it as a two-masted sailboat, which Dani thought had something to do with the math problem Mr. Parker was setting up (e.g., two seagoing vessels leave different ports at the same time, traveling 10 knots per hour . . .).

Dani also struggled in math because of the language required for explanation. Teachers explain math concepts and procedures, and students are required to explain how they get their answers. Both of these linguistic aspects of mathematics are often overlooked. Analyzing the amount of listening and speaking proficiency required to meet math objectives is not a typical part of many mathematics classrooms. An essential element of mathematics instruction for English learners is connecting math content to language, just as Mr. Parker eventually did with the assistance of the bilingual teacher.[10]

Family

In Iraq, Rebin and Azade were educated professionals who stressed intellectual development and academic achievement with their children. The Rebez family spoke Arabic at home, and Dani and Sevîn commuted to a bigger city to attend Arabic-medium schools, but older generations of their relatives spoke Kurdish as well as Arabic. When they left Iraq, Rebin spoke some English, which was self-taught, and Azade spoke no English, but despite the family's limited exposure to English before arriving in Texas, they valued education and encouraged one another to do well in their new schools. Because there were few English resources in Hiror, Rebin translated Dani's and Sevîn's school records. Unfortunately, his literal interpretation, which offered no evaluation of US course equivalents, contributed to the confusion about the credits Dani had completed.

With Rebin's full-time study at the English institute, there was little time left over for involvement in the everyday concerns of Dani and Sevîn. Azade attempted to meet those needs, but her lack of English hindered involvement at her children's schools. Dani pitched in to interpret during the meeting with Sevîn's teacher, which is a very common occurrence for English learner families. Where possible, it is beneficial for the school to provide interpretation through online services or district-level resources rather than depend on the EL child or their siblings.

Student

Dani started at Alcove High with a beginning level of English proficiency. He had previously studied English at school in Iraq, but only a few hours per week, and his classes focused on learning the grammar and some common, formulaic phrases, such as *How do you do?* Studying English in Iraq prepared him to communicate better than if he had had no previous exposure whatsoever, but understanding different accents and slang can be as challenging at first as understanding the language used in academic subjects. In *Educating English Learners*, my coauthors and I give an overview of the differences between instructed second language acquisition (i.e., studying the language) and naturalistic second language acquisition (i.e., picking up the language through immersion in a community that speaks it).[11] It's helpful for teachers to understand these distinctions, especially for secondary students like Dani. Dani is part of a group of English learners known as newcomers, which has different meanings but typically refers to ELs who have been in US schools for two years or less.[12]

Although Dani did well in mathematics and science back in Iraq, he did not enjoy reading in any language, which carried over to his reading development in English. This had an impact on his performance in English class as well as social studies, which required substantial reading and writing.

Struggles with cultural differences permeated Dani's introduction to life in the US, as in the instance of his degree of personal space in contrast to Mr. Parker's. Dani was teased about his accent and about his unfamiliarity with American culture and Texas traditions.[13] Because he had an outgoing personality and a vigorous sense of humor, these characteristics enabled him to connect with others once he developed adequate proficiency in English to communicate. In addition, his love of science and his passion for soccer provided connections with others and helped him maintain a sense of self-worth even under generally trying circumstances. Counselors, teachers, and coaches at Alcove High who recognized the assets Dani possessed were able to validate and build upon them to further his success.

DANI'S STORY DISCUSSION QUESTIONS

1. Dani had studied English in Iraq before coming to the US, but the amount of time he spent in English classes was minimal, and many of his teachers were not proficient in English themselves. Have you ever studied a language in school and then traveled (or moved) to a country that speaks the language? How well prepared did you feel? What advantages did having studied the language provide?
2. Dani's father was a graduate student in the US. How do you think Rebin's experience in the US higher education system affected Dani's experience in high school and beyond?
3. Dani used humor to make friends and cope with stressful situations. What types of humor translate well from one culture to another, and what types don't? How can humor be helpful for EL students, and when might it backfire?
4. Dani's classmates joked about his accent, something they thought was in good fun. How might imitating or commenting on someone's accent be hurtful? What might be a supportive way to clarify understanding if someone can't comprehend an EL student's accent?

5. Dani decided to let a school employee assume an inaccurate reason for his sister's refusal to eat certain foods. Did he do the right thing in leaving it at that? How else could he have handled the situation, and what might the result have been?
6. Dani's teacher thought that EL students from the same country would bond instantly. Why didn't Dani and Nawras hit it off? What other factors might cause compatriots to not get along or help one another?

CHAPTER 6

LOREDANA'S STORY

"COME ON! I WAS HERE FIRST!" Loredana hollered as a blue sedan whipped around the corner and took the last parking space in the lot. "That's not right!" she said as she slowly rolled past the wrongdoer, shaking her head exaggeratedly as he avoided eye contact.

It was 12:55, and Loredana's class started at 1:00. She'd been circling the lot for twenty minutes. Would it take twenty more before she could park? Her stomach was cramping. Ugh. Nerves again. She had spent so long trying to make it to college, and now, on her very first day, she was showing up late.

Caracas, Venezuela, was home to Loredana and her loud and large family of aunts, uncles, and cousins, so many cousins, fifteen of them, so far. Loredana was born and raised in Bello Campo, a neighborhood in a beautiful part of Caracas, on the east side, in a valley below a six-thousand-foot mountain called El Avila. Although everyone lived in different neighborhoods of the capital, Loredana's relatives got together nearly every week for Sunday dinners, rotating homes but most often gathering at either of her grandparents' places on the outskirts of the city, which had more space to let the grandkids roam. Not everybody went each week, naturally, but over the course of a month Loredana spent time with virtually every member of her entire family.

Loredana had always done well in school there, excelling in the humanities but also standing out for her skills in mathematics and science. She loved to read, she loved to write, and she loved to sing. Her mother, Ana, often told the story of little Loredana's first day at an afterschool music program, when her chorus teacher ran out to the sidewalk where Ana was waiting and gushed, "Your daughter has perfect pitch! Such a beautiful voice!" Ana didn't quite know how to respond, but simply said, "Thank you." She soon became accustomed to accepting many compliments for Loredana.

Life was good for Loredana and her family, until it wasn't. Everyone knew there had been a big political shift, but no one knew where it would lead. It wasn't like a full-blown catastrophe broke their lives apart instantaneously. It was incremental, a series of ominous events that made life become unbearable in their ancestral home. First was the nationalization of industries, then food shortages. By the time Ana and her husband, Carlos, decided to leave, they each carried concealed handguns to protect the family from kidnapping and murder. The crisis was moving in like a zoom lens, with the countryside hit hard before the majestic city of Caracas began to feel the brunt. Now the city markets' shelves were almost empty, and the cost of a bag of rice was a week's salary. All Loredana's cousins, aunts, uncles, and grandparents, as well as she, her mother, father, and little brother, would have to prepare to leave for good.

Loredana's extended family hoped to resettle somewhere collectively, and they felt clear-eyed about the process to reunite everyone in one place. They knew it wouldn't happen all at once. Some would make it out first, and others would join later. The reassembly of their family some place outside of Venezuela would occur over time, maybe a year, they thought.

Hedging his bets, Carlos had been applying for the US visa lottery ever since conditions took a turn for the worse. Everyone else in the extended family had done the same, a year or so later, as each followed their own timeline to recognize the direness of their predicament. Luckily, the odds favored Carlos, the only winner among them all, so he began the process of obtaining permanent resident status, which would enable him to bring Ana, Loredana, and her little brother, Luis. Soon they started planning the family's move to the United States.

As it turned out, the families of each of Loredana's aunts and uncles, as well as her grandparents, endured overwhelming challenges in finding a country to move to. Over the next three years, Carlos's parents moved to Spain, and Ana's relocated to Mexico. One aunt's family joined her parents in Madrid, and other aunts settled in New Zealand, Argentina, and Australia. Loredana's uncles' families were similarly scattered, with one in Panamá and one in Perú. And Loredana and her family started over in Los Angeles. There wasn't one big happy place that welcomed the whole family, after all. It took five continents to host their escape act.

Everybody knows that rent is expensive in Los Angeles, but the two-bedroom, one-bath bungalow that Loredana's family could afford in south LA was smaller than anticipated. Being crowded together in the eight-hundred-square-foot house intensified every problem they grappled with. The small dinette in the kitchen was where they hashed out most family issues.

> "How soon do you think we can find a bigger place, Papá?" Loredana asked and gestured to Luis to pass the salt.

"I think we'll be here for a while," Carlos replied.

"Why do *I* have to sleep on the porch? The vinyl enclosure makes it feel like a greenhouse, and the window air-conditioner isn't keeping it cool."

Carlos shrugged.

"I don't have a closet, and there's no room for anything but my bed and a nightstand. I'm fifteen years old. I should have my own room," Loredana complained, letting out a long burst of obstructed air from her lips—"ppffffff"—to punctuate her exasperation.

"We'll get a bigger place once we both get jobs," Ana said, encouragingly.

Luis smiled and nodded, but Loredana remained unconvinced.

Loredana's parents were entrepreneurs. The successful small business they used to own in Venezuela made plant-based soaps and detergents and had contracts with eco resorts near national parks and scenic attractions. Carlos had a business associate from back home who had established a tech startup in south Los Angeles, taking advantage of tax incentives for locating there, and he encouraged Carlos to move nearby so he could set up a business, too.

The last of the savings Carlos and Ana brought to LA would cover rent and living expenses for six months, but they weren't waiting to work until then. Unfortunately, Carlos didn't know anything about web design, so his Venezuelan friend couldn't employ him, and there were no investors to fund his eco-detergent-business idea in LA. So, he took on day-labor landscaping jobs and enrolled in a beginning English course at night. Once he was promoted to intermediate-level classes, he signed on as a rideshare driver, just until something better came along. It was a good move, though, because that's how he was able to buy a used Chevy Spark.

Since moving to LA, Loredana's mother, Ana, had developed chronic stomach pain, but she and Carlos didn't understand the health-care system in the US or whether they were covered for these sorts of contingencies, so she put off having it checked. She mostly stayed home, lying down because reclining eased her symptoms. To contribute to the family income, when Loredana and Luis were at school, she made handmade soap bars that a neighbor sold at his booth at a local farmer's market.

Loredana's high school years in LA had their ups and downs; actually, mostly downs. Thrust into an incomprehensible school culture, and learning in a language she couldn't understand, fifteen-year-old Loredana found herself as lost as if she were floating in outer space. The best that her teachers at Grammercy High could do was to pair her with another "Spanish speaker," but most of the buddies she was given didn't speak much Spanish and definitely not high school biology Spanish. Some of them resented being appointed a buddy. Who could blame them? They weren't being paid to teach.

Like many EL students, Loredana struggled because she started high school without the priceless asset of English. Until then, she had banked a valuable surplus of Spanish language assets, but they didn't add up to much here. Other than the Spanish for Spanish Speakers classes her counselor recommended, there were no courses she could take in Spanish, and all the academic knowledge she could display in her mother tongue wouldn't earn her one measly Carnegie unit.[1] It would be reasonable to assume that there were Latin American students at Grammercy High, peers Loredana could relate to. There were. But Loredana never had a class with a Venezuelan, and barely anyone could state even one simple fact about her country. She might as well have been from Vanuatu, as far as they were concerned.

Loredana's high school experience was, for the most part, a massive shock, like the unexpected blow of being rear-ended at a stoplight, except the wreck was continuous, for months on end. So, it was rather poignant that Loredana had previously held grand expectations for the American high school, having watched *Clueless* more than once, but there was no payoff for this Venezuelan newcomer's initial cheerful outlook. High school in California turned her into a different person.

The sun was rising later as Loredana's first quarter at Grammercy was wrapping up, so Carlos turned on the porch light to wake her for school.

"Good morning, Loredana! Time to get up!"

"OK, Papá."

"Come have breakfast with me before I head out."

"I'll be there in a minute."

Loredana picked her jeans up off the floor and put on a T-shirt.

"Didn't you wear that yesterday?" Carlos asked as Loredana sat down at the dinette.

"I guess so."

Carlos set her coffee on the table.

"Here, I bought this pastry for you at that Salvadoran bakery. It's your favorite!"

"I'm not hungry, but thanks."

"Hey, tomorrow morning we're planning on going to the Saturday market. Wanna come?"

"Sounds like fun, but I think I'll sleep in."

"You're missing out on some beautiful days, staying home sleeping every weekend."

"I know. I'd just rather sleep. I'm really tired."

Loredana continued on this way for the remainder of tenth grade, and eleventh grade proceeded similarly. As she acquired more English, she passed more classes, but that love of learning that was her trademark in Venezuela had dulled during her time at Grammercy High. She knew she had to finish high school and graduate from college like her parents did, and by this point she was making steady progress, but that old enthusiasm was gone.

In twelfth grade, though, life got better. At last, Loredana had room in her schedule to take electives, so she enrolled in a yearlong concert choir course. The lessons on vocal technique, music theory, and sight reading felt much like the afterschool music program she excelled in as a child. There were a lot of talented vocalists at Grammercy, but she could hold her own, and, almost magically, her accent disappeared when she sang in English. Finally, she felt at home.

The best part of class was when the choir practiced in formation. Loredana sang soprano, and she stood on the middle-left side of the stage, right next to the altos, where she could hear the harmonies blending notes. Sopranos can feel superior to altos, with the solos and all, but Loredana had no such pretensions. She was just happy to sing, and that made her approachable to the alto who stood next to her. Valeria was her name, and she was a third-generation Mexican American whose parents owned a successful hair salon near the school.

Loredana and Valeria became best friends, which opened up a whole new social life for Loredana. They spent most Saturdays venturing into downtown LA, the first time hanging out at the Day of the Dead festival on Olvera Street, other times watching movie scenes being shot on location, and many weekends just sampling snacks at the local favorite, Clifton's Cafeteria.

At the end of twelfth grade, Valeria was notified of her acceptance by UCLA to study voice, a great distinction because it only selects twelve students out of three hundred applicants each year. But the end of twelfth grade meant the beginning of thirteenth grade for Loredana, who needed an extra year to pass all her tests and graduate.

Around the time that Valeria got the notice, Loredana met with her school counselor to make college plans. She told him that she hoped to follow Valeria to UCLA. He scanned her transcript and said, bluntly, "Your pathway is through the community college."

Loredana looked down, paused a second, then responded.

"Why community college and not Stanford, or Harvard? I'll be *nineteen* by the time I graduate high school. I used to be smart. It's just taken me a while to prove that here."

On her first day at the new campus, after giving up on finding a space, Loredana parked illegally on the median of the entrance to Robles Community College. Arms filled with books and notebooks, she made her way into Building D, ran up three flights of stairs, then turned left. About halfway down the hallway was room 304, and she could see through the door pane that class was in full swing. She gripped the handle and turned her fist clockwise, slowly enough to keep the clicks quiet as the latch released. Pushing against the heavy, spring-loaded hinge with minimal force, she smiled awkwardly as a few students turned to see who was coming in late.

On the whiteboard was printed, "ENG 1070: First Year Composition Prof. Stoddard." Roll had been taken, and Ms. Stoddard was explaining their assignment, due before the next class. Loredana sat down and started taking notes. "You will write a five-hundred-word, typed, double-spaced essay, responding to this question 'Which is more important? Talent or hard work?'"

From the look of things, without the scarcest acknowledgment, let alone welcome, from Ms. Stoddard, Loredana knew she had gotten off on the wrong foot. No one told her that she needed to arrive on campus an hour early. That's not how it was in high school. All she could do now was make the best of it and start working on the first assignment.

Over the weekend, Loredana tackled her first writing assignment seriously, even if she was short on time because of her job at In-N-Out Burger. Ms. Stoddard's directions were clear, and the resources on constructing an argument were helpful, so Loredana dug in and sketched out a plan. On Saturday morning, using the library's database, she found ten sources about talent and diligence. As she read through the articles, she created a classic outline of their points to guide her writing. Then she reflected on the main argument she wanted to make, drawing a flowchart to show how it would unfold. Sunday was dedicated to her first draft, and she followed the checklist for all the required elements: opening paragraph that summarizes the subject and key points—check; engaging topic sentence—check; body of text in logical order—check; everything properly cited—check; conclusion that wraps everything up concisely and clearly—check; 500 words—check, but actually 580. She let the draft rest while she worked the day shift on Monday, then she did a cold read Monday night and caught a few things. When the whole composition was sufficiently polished, on Tuesday morning, a couple hours before the deadline, she uploaded her completed assignment to the course's website. After the next class, her grade appeared: 61 out of 100. Could it be that bad?

Loredana opened the essay file, which was now resaved, including her instructor's comments. With it, Ms. Stoddard had attached a handout listing the error codes that she typed in the comment boxes next to each problematic line of the text.

> *Faulty sentence structure (FS)*
> *Unnecessary shifts in verb tense (VT)*
> *Comma splices (CS)*
> *Sentence fragments (SF)*

Loredana read her topic sentence and the next few lines.

> Sometimes talent and hard work aren't enough to succeed...

OK, so far, so good.

By the fourth line, a code was waiting for this sentence:

> I could have went to a university if I didn't begun high school with no English.

VT x2!! screamed the comments box. Ouch. That code looked annoyed. Down to the next box, by this sentence:

> Why working hard is the goal for most people in US succeed?" **FS**

And by the five-hundredth word, there were another two **FS**s and one **CS** and one **SF**.

At the bottom was an invitation, or an order: "See me about this paper during my next office hours." Loredana decided to make a special trip to campus the next day to take care of this.

Shortly after the building opened, Loredana walked down the hallway and waited there until another student left Ms. Stoddard's office. When it was her turn, Loredana identified herself, and Ms. Stoddard pulled up her work on the computer, looking at her so disappointedly.

> "Loredana, this is sloppy, first-draft, unproofread work. You need to read what you write before you turn it in. It's full of mistakes."
>
> Loredana's heart sank.
>
> "I read it carefully. I tried my best," she countered. "English is my second language."
>
> "Well, then, you don't belong in *this* course. Come back after you learn English," Ms. Stoddard said, dismissively.

Loredana thought she *was* learning English. Wasn't that the point of the course? Just because she graduated from Grammercy High School didn't mean she was all done learning English, did it?

> "I know we don't have remedial courses anymore," Ms. Stoddard continued, "but Cal State Long Beach has an ESL program. That's the best place for you."
>
> Loredana did a double take.
>
> "That's for international students! I graduated from high school here."
>
> Ms. Stoddard wasn't having it.
>
> "You should have learned this in high school, Loredana."

Loredana kept trying to improve, asking Valeria to review her papers before she submitted them. That helped her grades somewhat, but with proctored exams, when she didn't have a native speaker to correct her grammar before she turned them in, she did very poorly.

All her hard work basically got her nowhere. She finished Comp 1 with a C minus, and a C was required to pass.

Loredana's little brother, Luis, had become a tall fifth grader, taller than his mother, Ana, and more proficient in English by far. He accompanied Ana on errands and school visits to interpret for her when Loredana was in class or at work, and he had become well aware of the changing power differential now that he was an upperclassman at his elementary school.

Fifth grade brought other changes, namely the drop in Luis's grades and the stagnation of his standardized test scores. Luis was also tardy more frequently because he wouldn't mind Ana when she tried to get him up and ready on time for school. His teacher was concerned that he was not on track for reclassification to *former* EL student by the end of the year, his fifth year of being an English learner, a critical point that coincided with the great transition of moving into middle school. Luis's teacher felt that he and his family were overdue in turning this trend around.

Loredana was a casual observer of Luis's maturation, but she couldn't miss the tension that was building between him and their mother. With all that was going on during her first semester in college, adding Luis's troubles to her own was an overwhelming notion. But Loredana did what a good big sister should and talked with him one day after school.

> "Hey, Mamá mentioned that your teacher contacted her about your grades."
>
> Luis gave his sister the side eye, then answered almost inaudibly.
>
> "Yeah."
>
> "What's that about?"
>
> "I messed up on a couple tests."
>
> Loredana folded her arms and leaned back and to the left, raising her eyebrows suspiciously.
>
> "Mamá said some mornings you won't get up on time for school."
>
> "Just when I'm not feeling well. You know I get stomachaches."

Ana walked in, unnoticed, and unaware of the topic of their talk. She stayed back, quietly, and listened.

> "Well . . . ," Loredana responded. You know how hard Mamá and Papá work so we can get a good education."
>
> Luis looked down, slouching in a wilted sort of way.
>
> "Mamá doesn't feel well a lot of mornings, but she never misses a day of work at the bakery."
>
> Loredana looked at Luis, flicking her chin upward to prompt his agreement.
>
> "Papá drives people around the city all hours of the day and night, and now he's even taking business classes at my college to make our lives better. I had a hard

time in high school, and there were days when I wanted to give up, but everything Mamá and Papá taught us is too important to throw away."

Luis took a deep breath.

"Even kids from the best families struggle sometimes," Loredana encouraged Luis. "The important thing is to keep getting better at everything you're learning in school."

Luis flashed a shy smile and nodded.

"OK, so we're good? You got it?"

"We're good."

It would never have occurred to Ana to ask Loredana to talk with Luis about his behavior, but she knew that Luis heard it from his sister in a way he couldn't from his mom. Ana had worried so about Loredana when high school incrementally stripped her dignity away, but now she saw that same girl restoring their family's dignity in the eyes of her son.

The Museum of Latin American Art in Long Beach was festively decorated for the special event celebrating Latinx-owned businesses. Loredana and her family met up with Carlos's Venezuelan friend, the owners and employees of the Salvadoran bakery where Ana worked, and Valeria's family, proud entrepreneurs all. There were three tables together that no one had claimed yet, so they all sat down and began chatting in Spanish.

"I notice they call us Latin*x* businesses, Ana said. "That's not how we use the letter *x* in Spanish. That's just wrong!"

"It's a new trend—nonbinary language," offered a young employee from the bakery.

Valeria's grandfather interjected with mighty disapproval.

"No, no, Latin*x*! What is that? Some mutant English version of who we are. Our people say Latin*o*."

"Now, wait a minute," Loredana and Valeria spoke up for the youth.

"We proudly call ourselves Latin*x*. Those of us who are young trendsetters, that is," said Valeria.

"Yeah, we were spreading avocado on our toast way before it was cool!" Loredana joked.

"Right, and on our arepas and tortillas, too!" Valeria specified.

Everyone laughed, young and old alike. Loredana and Valeria continued their cultural comparisons.

"We had to get used to the American way of doing things, though. When we first got here from Venezuela, Mamá thought the cashier at Marshalls cheated her because the bill was ten percent more than what the tag said!"

"Yeah, our sales tax rates are high in LA!" Valeria affirmed.

Loredana went on.

"And tipping! What's that all about, right? Ten percent if they're terrible, fifteen if they're OK, twenty if they're good—who made that up? And what about the big question everyone asks you here that they don't want you to answer?"

"Huh?" asked Valeria.

"*How are you?* Well, actually I've learned that there's only one right answer. Good, and you?" said Loredana.

Some members of their multifamily group nodded knowingly, while others nodded like they got it for the first time, an *aha!* about their own culture.

"We don't notice those American quirks because we grew up with them, but I'm sure they seem weird to people from other countries," said Valeria, summing it all up.

"Well, we Latinxs may not see everything the same way," Carlos said with a grin, exaggeratedly tripping over the *nxs* blend, "but we are alike in so many ways. Our Venezuelan family is spread all over the world, but one thing each relative does, from every corner of the planet, is provide for and take care of our parents. We're very proud of that."

"Yes, we do the same," Valeria's mother added, looking over at her elderly parents, who nodded approvingly.

"Family comes first."

"And no matter what happens, we help each other. Familia es familia," said Valeria.[2]

"Familia es familia," the group stated in agreement, almost in unison.

And "amor es amor," said Loredana.

Carlos repeated, rather automatically, "amor es amor," continuing the collective call and response just as he had done before with "familia es familia." But then, Carlos abruptly looked straight at Loredana and let out an imperceptible, tiny gasp. In that instant, when time paused indefinitely, Carlos saw Loredana looking back at him, tenderly, and he let his gaze soften, transforming his countenance from startled to content.

"Sí, amor es amor," he affirmed with a slow, gracious, diagonal nod, and he meant it. So did everyone else.

There was a flurry of activity at Robles CC, the kind that occurs when everyone's trying to complete all their tasks before the semester ends. The faculty lounge was standing room only, as many instructors were letting off steam while drinking weak coffee, after marathon grading sessions in their offices and at home. Ms. Stoddard, the standard-bearer of Composition 1, liked to chat with another comp instructor, Ms. Jefferson, and today they were entertaining each other with stories about the semester's challenges and successes.

"I think I have a student who took your course last semester," Ms. Jefferson said.

"Oh yeah? How do you know?"

"For the assignment where they write about a hardship in their life and how they overcame it, the student mentioned your class!"

Ms. Stoddard looked intrigued, yet mildly annoyed. "Oh, that's great," she said sarcastically. "So, I'm the hardship?!"

"No, no! I didn't mean that! She wrote about the turmoil in Venezuela and how her family had to leave and start over here." Ms. Jefferson exaggerated her positive tone and cheerful expression to compensate for any negative impressions made.

"So, how did I come into the picture?"

"Well . . ." Ms. Jefferson stretched out her favorite filler. "Loredana, that's her name, she wrote about having to learn English in high school and then struggling her first semester in college."

Ms. Stoddard looked on skeptically.

"And she said that just like with high school, it took some time for her to figure out how college works, but now she's doing better and feels more successful this semester."

Ms. Stoddard shrugged slightly, then laughed.

"She's lucky she got *you* this semester."

"Maybe I'm the lucky one," Ms. Jefferson opined. "I was impressed with her argument, and the insight of her closing sentence stayed with me. 'Sometimes hardship is a pathway to success.' Don't I know it!"

Ms. Stoddard nodded in agreement.

"Yeah, I've learned that lesson, too. A lot later than my freshman year in college, though. Good for her. Sounds like she's improved her writing this semester."

"Yep. She's doing well," Ms. Jefferson confirmed.

A rare and record-breaking May rainstorm kept the skies gray and streets wet for the last couple days of the semester. It was easier to study when there was no reason to be outdoors, so Loredana was making one final push to finish her papers and prepare for exams. Her second semester at Robles had gone more smoothly than the first, and now that the end of the term was near, it seemed that she would pass all three of her classes—Environmental Science, College Algebra, and the stubborn ENG 1070, which she had to experience a second time.

Two days after finals, right when grades posted, Loredana logged on to see the results—an A in science, an A minus in algebra, and a B, a solid B, in composition! She called Valeria with the good news.

"I'm conquering Gen Ed! Woo!" Loredana cheered. "An A, an A minus, and a B!"

"You're amazing, Loredana! You passed Comp 1, you earned two As, and the sun is shining again."

"I'm so glad the semester is over," Loredana remarked.

"That ramen noodle place in Seal Beach has a lunch special on Saturdays. Let's go celebrate your grades, my treat!" offered Valeria.

After lunch, they left the car in the shopping center lot and went for a stroll. They loved walking along the quaint Main Street USA downtown, lined with gourmet stores selling California olive oil products and ice cream parlors that make date shakes. Main Street ended on the actual beach, whose centerpiece is a long fishing pier. Surfers flanked both sides of the pilings, as the storm that had brought the rain was now churning up some pretty impressive waves. Valeria and Loredana laid out a towel parallel to the beach and sat there, mesmerized.

On the distant horizon, well beyond the surfers, Loredana noticed offshore oil rigs, as tall as skyscrapers set into the ocean floor, but the size of Erector Set models, from her perspective. Closer in, several empty cans and bottles floated on the water's surface, pushing closer to the shore with every wave. The stormwater runoff had deposited litter into the ocean, but that didn't deter the surfers, and neither did the huge concrete platforms out at sea. They couldn't have been more stoked, even if they were riding the Hawaiian-scale swells of tropical Waimea Bay. Loredana watched them studiously. Some bobbed, straddling their boards, hopping up quickly for the next surging wave, only to be knocked off unceremoniously. Others sat a few waves out, then got up for the next promising one, or the one after that, gliding in toward the sand, turning around and paddling back out, doing it all over again. There were first-timers and every-Saturday surfers, grandparents and grandchildren, and groups of teens hanging out without adult supervision, probably for the first time. Maybe even be a few professionals in the making.

For a moment, Loredana imagined herself out there, feeling that forward propulsion, the mighty force of the Pacific Ocean that carried the surfers to shore. She felt herself firmly planted on the board, leaning into bottom turns, twisting back and forth repeatedly to ride the wave all the way down the line. It took talent and hard work, but she leaned into each wave, letting those individual qualities fully express through a ceaseless, unpredictable, and fluid momentum, a push from outside of herself, coupled with the drive within.

A gust of wind toppled a nearby umbrella, redirecting Loredana's attention to the towel where she and Valeria sat.

> "It's easy to get lost in the moment on a day like this," Valeria told Loredana.
>
> "Oh, I'm not lost." Loredana said pointedly. "I know exactly where I am, and I love it."

EPILOGUE

Birth Home (or Family's Place of Origin) to US Home

Venezuela's landmass is approximately twice the size of California. Its land is bordered by Brazil, Colombia, and Guyana, and its coastline is on the Caribbean Sea and North Atlantic Ocean. Venezuela is known for some of the world's most beautiful waterfalls, especially Angel Falls, the highest anywhere. It also has tabletop mountains, the highest of which is over fifteen thousand feet, and a pristine, tropical archipelago called Los Roques. Venezuela's capital is Caracas, on the northern coast, and its climate is tropical, although the highlands are more moderate and less humid. Natural resources of Venezuela include petroleum, natural gas, and various minerals. Ninety-seven percent of its population of 28 million is literate, and 88 percent of its residents live in urban areas.[3]

Venezuela is a federal presidential republic in South America, governed by a president, Nicolas Maduro, that the United States does not recognize. The US Department of State recommends avoiding travel to Venezuela due to crime, civil unrest, poor health care, kidnapping, and arrest and detention of US citizens.[4]

Community in the United States

There are approximately 420,000 people in the US who identify as Venezuelan. Although the population of Venezuelans ranks thirteenth among people of Hispanic origin in the US, their numbers have recently increased precipitously, 352 percent since 2000.[5] In comparison, the largest group of Hispanic Americans in the US, 36 million people, originates from Mexico. South American immigrants are about 7 percent of the foreign-born residents of the US. The greatest numbers of immigrants from South America come from Columbia, at 24 percent, with Perú, Ecuador, and Brazil each at 14 percent, and Venezuela at 11 percent.[6]

Venezuelans in the US vary from the majority of Americans of Hispanic origin in multiple ways. Seventy-four percent of Venezuelans living in the US are foreign-born, compared to 33 percent of Hispanics in general. Sixteen percent of US Hispanics aged twenty-five plus possess a bachelor's degree, but 55 percent of Venezuelans do. Fifty-two percent of the US Venezuelan population lives in Florida, with their Texas population at 11 percent and New York at 4 percent. Sixty-four percent of Hispanic adults in the US are proficient in English, but 54 percent of Venezuelans are, which is likely due to their more recent immigration. Twenty-five percent of South American immigrants have settled in Florida, and 20 percent live in New York. Los Angeles County is among the top-five US counties in terms of South American immigrants.[7]

School

Robles Community College was like many educational institutions that serve their local community. Overall, it did a good job of addressing the majority of its students' needs, but there were gaps in how it met the needs of EL students. In general, schools for all ages that do an overall good job of meeting EL students' needs may employ teachers that don't, and schools that don't do an overall good job of meeting EL students' needs may employ teachers that do. That's one reason that EL students fall through the cracks, not progressing as expected or developing gaps in their skills and knowledge.

Loredana's experiences at Robles differed by course and semester, primarily because of how informed faculty were about second language writing and English learners' areas of development. Ms. Stoddard, who had years of experience, hadn't updated her composition instructional knowledge about second language writers like Loredana, known as Generation 1.5. A "yeah, but this is college . . ." outlook among faculty doesn't serve anyone's interests, as there is no such thing as a threshold that English learners clear, never to need support again.

In *Show, Tell, Build*, a book of instructional tools and techniques that I coauthored with four colleagues, we give specific guidance on supporting second language learners' writing, and on sentence-level errors like those in Loredana's first-semester composition in particular.[8] There are also equity-minded college composition instructors who provide sage advice online, explaining classroom-tested ways to respond to English learners' work. One of these instructors likened Generation 1.5 students' persistent grammatical errors to their spoken accents. Just as with speaking patterns, sentence-level grammar is affected by differences in the students' native language and English, and also by the age when they began learning English. Therefore, it's wrong to just assume that a student who submits papers with grammatical errors is lazy, or doesn't bother editing their work, or hasn't raised their command of English to some undefined college-level minimum by spending enough time studying about the language.[9] To address sentence-level errors, writing instructors need to be strategic in responding to those that English learners like Loredana make, selecting a few to concentrate on at a time, and providing instructional resources to elucidate the correct form. Instructors should not give excessive weight to a lack of grammatical errors in EL students' compositions because it discourages the risk-taking necessary to develop language proficiency. If Loredana had used simpler sentences, she probably wouldn't have made those grammatical errors. Errors should be used to help students learn, not as a penalty for taking a risk. And, very importantly, instructors need to give appropriate focus to how the Generation 1.5 student put together their argument, something that was neglected when Loredana's teacher responded with antipathy to her grammatical transgressions and failed her because of them.

Colleges and universities seeking to be more inclusive have increasing resources available. One helpful article entitled "Start the Semester Inclusively" suggests ways faculty can be more culturally responsive.[10] The authors' first suggestion is to become aware of one's own biases, searching through syllabi and readings for representation of different races and cultures. They also suggest surveying students before the semester begins to find out specifics such as their preferred pronouns and their access to technology. Expressing empathy for issues that are complicating their studies is an important way to be supportive. Another recommendation is to learn how to pronounce students' names, asking students to write them phonetically if needed, rather than joke about their difficulty.

Family

Carlos, Ana, Loredana, and Luis call their big Venezuelan family *nomads* because everyone lives in different parts of the world. Technology has been helpful for them to keep in touch with each other's lives, but everyone misses those Sunday get-togethers. None of the extended family members has been able to return to Venezuela since leaving. Carlos and Ana were eligible for the US Diversity Immigrant Visa lottery because they were Venezuelan citizens and had a minimum of a high school education. Only citizens of certain countries are eligible for the Diversity Immigrant Visa.[11]

Ana eventually felt comfortable enough about the health-care system that she went for routine checkups and followed recommendations that helped her stress-induced digestive issues. Subsequently, she started ESL classes at the adult education center near their new home, and after finishing the highest level, she plans to follow Carlos in earning a certificate of entrepreneurial studies at Robles CC. Using information that he learned in his classes, Carlos started meeting with small business development consultants to make a business plan to produce their soaps and detergents for socially responsible hotels in Southern California. The family is beginning the process to become American citizens, which will make more business opportunities and funding for college available. Most importantly, citizenship will make them eligible to freely elect their local, state, and national leaders after losing that cherished right during the political upheaval in Venezuela.

Student

Loredana fits a pattern of students sometimes referred to as Generation 1.5. These students are enrolled in higher education, were born in a non-English-speaking country, but have lived in the US for an extended period and are immigrants, not international students staying temporarily. They often speak English fluently but are still developing academic writing skills, even though they completed high school in the US.[12] In Loredana's case, she is a US high school graduate and attended secondary education in Los Angeles for four years before enrolling in community college. Loredana is typical of many Generation 1.5 students, and postsecondary educators are developing more guidance on how their needs are different from students born and raised in English-speaking homes and from international students.

In addition to grammar errors and misunderstandings, there are always aspects of the language and culture that Generation 1.5 students aren't familiar with, such as idioms, uncommon words, jokes, old TV shows, and so on. Someone can feel very much a part of their new culture and then be together with people who were born and raised there who are reminiscing about commonalities from their childhoods, such as old TV shows, and they suddenly feel like a newcomer again. Valeria likes to tell a story about when the principal at Grammercy caught them leaving campus at lunch. She told Loredana that leaving school wasn't permitted and that she would have to face the music. Loredana innocently said she didn't hear any music, and she couldn't understand what the music needed her face to do. The principal thought Loredana was being facetious, but because she had never heard that expression before, she took it literally. Even those who have been in the US for their entire adult lives can still run across a novel saying that they misunderstand. That's a wrap![13]

LOREDANA'S STORY DISCUSSION QUESTIONS

1. When a crisis occurs in a country, and leaving appears to be the best option, groups of exiles may depart in waves, with some leaving soon after signs of impending distress and others taking longer to get out. Why do you think some people are able to leave sooner than others? Why do you think some people choose to risk leaving and others choose to risk staying? Is it always a choice?
2. Loredana's family dispersed all over the world after leaving Venezuela. How do you think this is different from or similar to other immigrants' experiences? How is it different from or similar to the experiences of American-born families that are spread throughout the US?
3. Loredana went through a period of not wanting to eat, not caring about her appearance, and not wanting to get out of bed. Do you think these behaviors were symptoms of something more than difficulty adapting to her new country? Do you think her parents and teachers should have addressed these issues more directly?
4. Ms. Stoddard penalized Loredana harshly for her grammatical errors. How do you react when someone speaks or writes in an incorrect way? Have you ever questioned why you react the way you do?

5. Loredana told her little brother to do all the things she didn't do when she was in high school. Have you ever felt you were teaching other people things you hadn't learned well yourself? Can you be an effective mentor in those cases?
6. Loredana's experience changed when she found love. What role can love have in immigrant English learners' adaptation to their new life?

CONCLUSION

AFTER GETTING TO KNOW RAFAEL, Dibenesha, Josué, Anh, Dani, and Loredana, it's time to reflect on what the stories told *you*. I hope that as you read each chapter, you could move into the space of the stories and keep time with the ongoing, but-often-uneven beat that leads the students toward glimpses of a better future. In the story chapters, you met many good actors who drummed up the energy, enthusiasm, encouragement, expectations, dedication, diligence, and resources needed to keep that beat steady. Will you be one of the influencers of achievement for English learners in your community?

TAKEAWAY THEMES ACROSS THE STORIES

Each of the six chapters included an epilogue that provided additional information and resources about the topics the story addressed, so this conclusion chapter takes a broad look at themes that cut across all or many of the stories. What follows is a summary of the themes gleaned from analysis of the text, key conclusions we can draw from the stories told in this book. Accordingly, some of these themes are derived from anecdotes shared with me by my students and colleagues, and from my own experiences, that found their way into the stories, and others come from research about English learners and immigrant students. I invite you to map these themes back to the characters and events in the stories as a way to engage more deeply with the book's takeaways. I hope the essence of the following insights will stay with you once you close this book.

Immigration Experiences

All stories in this book affirm that immigrants renew and reform American ideals, continuously replenishing our people's energy, drive, and optimism, moving us closer to the realization of our highest values and goals. Specific themes in this area include:

- EL students and their immigrant families can be a source of inspiration for all students.
- There are many paths for the families of English learners to move in the US, but it can be nearly impossible for people from certain countries and circumstances to immigrate here.
- Joining an extended immigrant family that is already in the US provides orientation and stability in many cases, but not always.
- Some families don't start out intending to be immigrants, but they can end up making the place they moved to temporarily their permanent home.
- The place where families of ELs settle affects their adjustment process. If it includes a community of people from similar backgrounds, there are opportunities for those who have been in the US longer to help newcomers.
- Religious and cultural organizations can be a means of support and connection for immigrant families. Leaders of these groups can be great informants and liaisons for schools, but not all EL families belong to such groups, so there is no shortcut for connection with each child's family.

Language Development

Many stories in this book offer insights into learning in two languages, and learning subjects in a new language at the same time as learning the language and about the language. This is a hallmark of English learners' experiences. Additional themes related to language development include:

- Becoming bilingual, biliterate, and bicultural is a valuable goal for all students, and equally so for English learners.
- Developing proficiency in the student's home language promotes their proficiency in the second language (English, for EL students).
- Children can learn their home language and English at the same time or in sequence.
- The higher the grade (i.e., kindergarten, first grade, and so on), the tougher the language barrier.
- The lower the student's English proficiency, the higher the climb to catch up.
- EL students' oral proficiency and literacy often are at different levels.
- An English learner's age when arriving in an English-speaking community, or when beginning formal study of English as a new language, affects the process and outcome of English language development.
- Prior study of English in the home country helps, to a point. There's a difference in having only studied the language as a course in school, and picking up the language by living where it is spoken.

- English learners can be at, or between, beginning, intermediate, or advanced levels of English proficiency, which are divided and specified in different ways depending on a state's chosen standards.
- Younger ELs acquire a second language in similar and different ways from older ELs. The spoken accent (influenced by first-language sounds) of ELs in secondary programs generally persists over time, while it diminishes for younger students (and even disappears for those in primary grades and below). The same can be true with other aspects of the language, such as the correctness of grammatical word forms and sentence structure.
- Every subject depends on the language skills of students for them to succeed, but some subjects depend more on language skills for student success than others.
- Attaining grade-level writing proficiency in a second language (in English, for EL students) may take longer than attaining equivalent proficiency in other language skills, such as reading or listening.

Student Progress and Achievement

Constant and consistent attention to English learners' progress in English language development and academic subject achievement is crucial. From the stories we have seen that educators can support that goal in numerous ways:

- Teachers will be more successful in fostering English learners' achievement if they know them well.
- Teachers will be more successful in fostering English learners' achievement if they work together with other teachers and educators.
- Applying EL students' talents in the arts, sports, and music can help them feel successful while learning English.
- So-called long-term English learners (LTELs) are at risk for not completing high school. It's very important to monitor and provide support that enables them to reach grade-level English language standards. We can see the causes and effects of this from the earliest grades through high school and beyond.

Student Access/Equity

English learners may lack some of the opportunities that other students enjoy, sometimes because of the assumption that they need to know English to be able to do X, Y, or Z. Teachers can question that assumption and seek ways to obtain the same opportunity perhaps in a different way. We've read examples of the following issues of access and equity:

- English learners can show signs of giftedness and/or learning difficulties that may be obscured or mitigated by language.
- Standardized testing policies differ by state for ELs, and some policies are not equitable for EL students.
- Assessment can be culturally and/or linguistically biased. Assessment intended specifically for EL students is an important means of monitoring language development, but even this type of language assessment is subject to bias.
- Different program models lead to different outcomes for ELs, but not all ELs have access to promising options, such as dual language education that includes their home language.
- The age at which an EL starts school in the US, and the quality of instruction, impact their career choices and high school completion rates.

Characteristics of English Learners

The six stories are a small fraction of the wide palette of English learner characteristics and experiences. For instance, large school systems in the US enroll English learners with as many as 175 different first languages. Here are some characteristics portrayed in the stories about our six English learners:

- English learners bring a wealth of cultural and linguistic assets to every classroom.
- English learners can be born in the US and begin preschool or kindergarten without having been exposed to English.
- English learners can begin school in the US at any grade.
- Socioeconomic status and parent(s)' level of education affect EL students' academic achievement as they do for non-EL students, to a point.
- Problems at home, such as financial insecurity (e.g., evictions, power turned off, and so on) and family members' health, safety, and relationships (e.g., the divorce of parents) affect EL students' academic achievement as with non-EL students, but immigration stress, developing English skills, and learning new systems can magnify the effect for ELs.
- Socioemotional learning for ELs encompasses everything it does for all students as well as issues specific to immigrant families and students.
- The degree of education and literacy in the home country/language impacts EL students' academic achievement in US classrooms.
- Interrupted schooling can occur with ELs for various reasons and in various ways, such as ending school when very young in their home country and moving to the US years later, moving back and forth between the US and the home country, and so on.

- English learners may struggle with feelings of being lost, out of their element, or an outsider, especially during their first years in US schools.

Understanding Cultural Similarities and Differences

Doing the work of understanding one's own culture as well as other cultures is a lifelong process, but one with many rewards. Cultural misunderstandings played a role in a number of the difficulties our six EL students experienced:

- Teachers should question stereotypes about countries and cultures and find facts about the specific ethnicities and cultures that their students are part of (i.e., ethnicity alone doesn't capture national or regional particularities, and nationality alone doesn't capture regional or cultural particularities). Teachers should also not assume that each individual acts or believes as the majority of their country is reported to.
- Rules and processes in US communities are different from those at home for many immigrants. It's natural to assume that institutions and regulations work like they do where you're from, but that assumption can lead to problems.
- EL students and their families can experience instances of discrimination, prejudice, and unconscious bias based on their race, ethnicity, culture, religion, first language, and English proficiency.[1]
- Learning to say EL students' names is a sign of respect and appreciation.
- Students and their families can experience disconnects and even collisions between the home and school spheres due to differences between the home culture and the culture of the community where they relocated (which is reflected in the school culture).

STEPS YOU CAN TAKE

For teachers doing the best that they can for their English learners, becoming more informed about these students and their families can make *the best that teachers can do* even better. In taking that extra step to learn about their students' home countries, cultures, languages, and immigration experiences, teachers can help shape each EL student's story.

Information teachers can look up to better understand their EL students

- If students have gone to school in another country (or territory) before starting school in the US, it's important to know some basic information about the educational system where they came from. Even if the student is

entering school for the first time, knowing something about the school system in their place of family origin will help you understand parents' expectations and behaviors.
- Knowing some of the history and geography of the student's or family's country or region of origin can help make connections with students.
- Learning current facts about the student's or family's country or region of origin can help with understanding their emotional states (e.g., wars in their region).
- Saying a few phrases and words in the student's or family's home language and acquiring some basic knowledge about that language (e.g., whether it uses the Roman alphabet, how different it is from English, etc.) shows an interest in the language assets EL students bring to class.

Information teachers can obtain from coworkers, students, students' families, and community representatives to better understand their EL students

- If a student's English proficiency levels have not been provided to the classroom teacher, ask the ESOL/ELD teacher (if the school has one) or an administrator or staff person responsible for student testing data. There are many resources that provide guidance for adapting instruction to students' English proficiency levels.[2]
- Talk with the EL student (with an interpreter, if needed) about their life before coming to the US. What was their best subject in school? How did they spend their free time? How is that different now? If they were born here, talk with them about their routines and who in their life speaks what languages.
- Speak with parents about the student's academic strengths and weaknesses when they were studying in their home country. Ask them how the student learns best and what motivates them.
- Ask community representatives about the struggles and successes that families experience with their children's achievement in school. Solicit ideas for how the school could connect better with the community.

Now that we have looked at themes and summarized key insights from the previous chapters, there are yet other story elements that can be critically analyzed from a variety of disciplinary lenses. If you find something in a story that resonates with you, or that you can relate to research or theory or best practices that you know of, please share that on the book website, https://englishlearnerachievement.com. That is one way we can keep the reflection and discussion going.

IN CONCLUSION: PEOPLE MAKE THE DIFFERENCE

Because I love spending time with people from different cultures, I've often been asked who my people are, and the best answer I could give is *teachers*. Teachers who commit to the profession, who give it all they've got, are my people. Lesson-planning, weekend-grading, record-keeping, awe-inspiring encouragers of schoolchildren big and small fill me with admiration of their daily heroics. Cultural studies scholar Henry Giroux describes teachers as *public intellectuals*, members of society that point us toward bigger ideas and better understandings.[3] They spend an entire semester, or school year, getting to know a group of growing individuals, releasing them into the wild of the next grade, better for it. They spend their professional lives nurturing the potential of generations who will grow up to be in charge of life as we know it. Not everyone is cut out for the teaching life, but those who are dedicated to it make their mark through what they enable others to accomplish. As a wise Latino once said, "the sun doesn't shine on itself"; similarly, a teacher's light amplifies the light of a student, helping them shine more brightly.[4]

You've probably already realized that teaching English learners, or any students for that matter, is a lot about giving. We can get worn down, giving so much of ourselves, but it's a fortunate position to be in, if you think about it. And there's no way to ascertain whether we receive as much as we give, especially because so much of what we get is intangible. But determining if what is exchanged between teachers and their students is equivalent isn't the point. Teaching isn't transactional. It's transformational. As we've seen in these stories, this is true for the teacher and the students, in roughly equal measure.

NOTES

Introduction

1. This book focuses on students who have been classified as English learners at some point in their PreK–12 school experiences. Students who are bilingual and/or bicultural but who have never been classified as English learners are outside of the scope of this book, although educators need to understand their backgrounds and needs as well. There are many good books focusing on Latinx, Asian, and other students from various home and heritage languages and cultural backgrounds.

   According to the Elementary and Secondary Education Act 8101(20):

   The term "English learner," when used with respect to an individual, means an individual—

   (A) who is aged 3 through 21;

   (B) who is enrolled or preparing to enroll in an elementary school or secondary school;

   (C)(i) who was not born in the United States or whose native language is a language other than English;

   (ii)(I) who is a Native American or Alaska Native, or a native resident of the outlying areas; and

   (II) who comes from an environment where a language other than English has had a significant impact on the individual's level of English language proficiency; or

   (iii) who is migratory, whose native language is a language other than English, and who comes from an environment where a language other than English is dominant; and

   (D) whose difficulties in speaking, reading, writing, or understanding the English language may be sufficient to deny the individual—

   (i) the ability to meet the challenging State academic standards;

   (ii) the ability to successfully achieve in classrooms where the language of instruction is English; or

   (iii) the opportunity to participate fully in society.

   Many terms are used for students who are, have been, or have similarities with English learners. Some current names for these students are emergent bilinguals, multilingual students, and dual language learners. While these identifiers could include the criteria listed above, they could also refer to students whose first language is English and are enrolled in dual language or world (also known as foreign) language immersion programs. To be clear about the subjects of this book, I use the US Department of Education term *English learner*.

2. The stories tell essential truths, even if some of the details are fictionalized.
3. Matthew Lavery, Joyce Nutta, and Alison Youngblood, "Analyzing Student Learning Gains to Evaluate Differentiated Teacher Preparation for Fostering English Learners' Achievement in Linguistically Diverse Classrooms," *Journal of Teacher Education* 70, no. 4 (September-October 2019): 372–387.
4. Generally speaking, this book uses the terms ESOL and ELD interchangeably to describe specialized classes that are offered exclusively for English learners because different states prefer one or the other (or sometimes both). English as a Second Language (ESL) is used in the book when describing the same type of course but for the postsecondary level.
5. Joyce W. Nutta, Kouider Mokhtari, and Carine Strebel, *Preparing Every Teacher to Reach English Learners: A Practical Guide for Teacher Educators* (Cambridge, MA: Harvard Education Press, 2012).
6. Joyce W. Nutta, Carine Strebel, Kouider Mokhtari, Florin M. Mihai, and Edwidge Crevecoeur-Bryant, *Educating English Learners: What Every Classroom Teacher Needs to Know* (Cambridge, MA: Harvard Education Press, 2014).
7. Joyce W. Nutta, Carine Strebel, Florin M. Mihai, Edwidge Crevecoeur Bryant, and Kouider Mokhtari, *Show, Tell, Build: Twenty Key Instructional Tools and Techniques for Educating English Learners* (Cambridge, MA: Harvard Education Press, 2018).
8. Some of the questions were adapted from the article "The Best Book Club Questions to Spark Discussion" by Elena Nicolaou, which has a lot of great suggestions for fiction and nonfiction book discussions. https://www.oprahmag.com/entertainment/a31047508/book-club-questions/.

Chapter 1

1. "Cuba," The World Factbook, Central Intelligence Agency, January 4, 2021, https://www.cia.gov/the-world-factbook/countries/cuba/.
2. "Cuba," The World Factbook, Central Intelligence Agency, December 2019, https://www.cia.gov/the-world-factbook/static/9008f7b26a3cf82a8ab1baa40a3e8a1d/CU-summary.pdf.
3. Mimi Whitefield, "Study: Cubans don't make much, but it's more than state salaries indicate," *Miami Herald*, July 12, 2016, https://www.miamiherald.com/news/nation-world/world/americas/cuba/article89133407.html.
4. Jorge Duany, "Cuban Migration: A Postrevolution Exodus Ebbs and Flows," Migration Policy Institute, July 6, 2017, https://www.migrationpolicy.org/article/cuban-migration-postrevolution-exodus-ebbs-and-flows.
5. Luis Noe-Bustamante, Antonio Flores, and Sono Shah, "Facts on Hispanics of Cuban origin in the United States, 2017," Pew Research Center Hispanic Trends, September 16, 2019, https://www.pewresearch.org/hispanic/fact-sheet/u-s-hispanics-facts-on-cuban-origin-latinos/.
6. "What Does the Research Really Say About Preschool Effectiveness?," Learning Policy Institute, January 31, 2019, https://learningpolicyinstitute.org/press-release/what-does-research-really-say-about-preschool-effectiveness.
7. Dana Charles McCoy et al., "Impacts of Early Childhood Education on Medium- and Long-Term Educational Outcomes," *Educational Researcher*, November 2017, https://journals.sagepub.com/doi/pdf/10.3102/0013189X17737739.

8. As reported in: "Dual Language Education Programs: Current State Policies and Practices," US Department of Education, Office of English Language Acquisition, 2015, https://www.air.org/sites/default/files/downloads/report/Dual-Language-Education-Programs-Current-State-Policies-April-2015.pdf; Office of English Language Acquisition, US Department of Education, May 22, 2020, http://www2.ed.gov/about/offices/list/oela/resources.html; Delia Silva Gómez, "Bridging the Opportunity Gap Through Dual Language Education," Dissertation Presented to the Faculty of California State University, Stanislaus, 2013, http://scholarworks.csustan.edu/bitstream/handle/011235813/658/GomezD%20Summer%202013.pdf?sequence=1; Kathryn Lindholm-Leary and Nicholas Block, "Achievement in predominately low SES/Hispanic dual language schools, *International Journal of Bilingual Education and Bilingualism* (2010), https://www.researchgate.net/publication/249024870_Achievement_in_predominantly_low_SESHispanic_dual_language_schools; Viorica Marian, Anthony Shook, and Scott R. Schroeder, "Bilingual Two-Way Immersion Programs Benefit Academic Achievement," *Bilingual Research Journal*, National Association for Bilingual Education, 2013, https://bilingualism.soc.northwestern.edu/wpcontent/uploads/2013/10/MarianetalImmersionEducation.pdf.
9. Anya Kamenetz, "6 Potential Brain Benefits Of Bilingual Education," NPR Ed, November 29, 2016, https://www.npr.org/sections/ed/2016/11/29/497943749/6-potential-brain-benefits-of-bilingual-education.
10. Joyce W. Nutta et al., *Educating English Learners: What Every Classroom Teacher Needs to Know* (Cambridge, MA: Harvard Education Press, 2014).
11. Karen Ford and Rebecca Palacios, "Early Literacy Instruction in Spanish: Teaching the Beginning Reader," Colorín Colorado, 2015, https://www.colorincolorado.org/article/early-literacy-instruction-spanish-teaching-beginning-reader.

Chapter 2

1. "Democratic Republic of the Congo," The World Factbook, Central Intelligence Agency, January 4, 2021, https://www.cia.gov/the-world-factbook/countries/congo-democratic-republic-of-the/.
2. "DR Congo Emergency," UNHCR, The UN Refugee Agency, March 2020, https://www.unhcr.org/en-us/dr-congo-emergency.html.
3. "What is a Refugee?," USA for UNHCR, The UN Refugee Agency, January 4, 2021, https://www.unrefugees.org/refugee-facts/what-is-a-refugee/.
4. "Refugees," US Citizenship and Immigration Services, May 7, 2020, https://www.uscis.gov/humanitarian/refugees-and-asylum/refugees.
5. Administration for Children & Families, Office of Refugee Resettlement, US Department of Health and Human Services, January 4, 2021, https://www.acf.hhs.gov/orr.
6. Church World Service (CWS), Ethiopian Community Development Council (ECDC), Episcopal Migration Ministries (EMM), Hebrew Immigrant Aid Society (HIAS), International Rescue Committee (IRC), US Committee for Refugees and Immigrants (USCRI), Lutheran Immigration and Refugee Services (LIRS), United States Conference of Catholic Bishops (USCCB), and World Relief Corporation (WR).
7. Joyce W. Nutta et al., *Show, Tell, Build: Twenty Key Instructional Tools and Techniques for Educating English Learners* (Cambridge, MA: Harvard Education Press, 2018).

8. The Schoolwide Enrichment Model (SEM), Renzulli Center for Creativity, Gifted Education, and Talent Development, January 4, 2021, https://gifted.uconn.edu/schoolwide-enrichment-model/.
9. "15 Tips for Identifying Gifted EL Students," National Center for Research on Gifted Education, January 4, 2021, https://ncrge.uconn.edu/wp-content/uploads/sites/982/2018/06/15-Tips.pdf.
10. "Tips for Identifying Gifted EL Students," The National Center for Research on Gifted Education, January 4, 2021, https://ncrge.uconn.edu/wp-content/uploads/sites/982/2018/06/Brochure.pdf.
11. Joyce W. Nutta et al., *Educating English Learners: What Every Classroom Teacher Needs to Know* (Cambridge, MA: Harvard Education Press, 2014).
12. "Mass Violence Resources," The National Child Traumatic Stress Network, January 4, 2021, https://www.nctsn.org/what-is-child-trauma/trauma-types/terrorism-and-violence/mass-violence.

Chapter 3

1. They never actually married, but soon after reuniting in the US, they started referring to each other as husband and wife.
2. "Mexico," The World Factbook, Central Intelligence Agency, January 19, 2021, https://www.cia.gov/the-world-factbook/countries/mexico/.
3. "The Indigenous World 2020," The International Work Group for Indigenous Affairs (IWGIA), April 2020, http://iwgia.org/images/yearbook/2020/IWGIA_The_Indigenous_World_2020.pdf.
4. "Indigenous Latin America in the Twenty-First Century, The First Decade," World Bank Group, 2015, http://documents1.worldbank.org/curated/en/145891467991974540/pdf/Indigenous-Latin-America-in-the-twenty-first-century-the-first-decade.pdf.
5. "The Indigenous World 2020," The International Work Group for Indigenous Affairs (IWGIA).
6. Allison O'Connor, Jeanne Batalova, and Jessica Bolter, "Central American Immigrants in the United States," Migration Policy Institute, August 15, 2019, https://www.migrationpolicy.org/article/central-american-immigrants-united-states-2017.
7. "Maya," History.com, January 29, 2021, https://www.history.com/topics/ancient-americas/maya.
8. An excellent book that chronicles the journey of a boy from Guatemala to the US is Sonia Nazario, *Enrique's Journey: The Story of a Boy's Dangerous Odyssey to Reunite with His Mother* (New York: Random House, 2014).
9. "Albergues," Red DH Migrantes, January 29, 2021, https://reddhmigrantes.wordpress.com/albergues/.
10. "Mayan Scientific Achievements," History.com, February 24, 2020, https://www.history.com/topics/ancient-americas/mayan-scientific-achievements.
11. "Who invented the zero?," History.com, August 22, 2018, https://www.history.com/news/who-invented-the-zero.
12. "The Maya People," Living Maya Time, Sun, Corn, and the Calendar, National Museum of the American Indian, Smithsonian Latino Center, 2021, https://maya.nmai.si.edu/the-maya/maya-people.

13. "H-2A Visa Program," US Department of Agriculture, January 29, 2021, https://www.farmers.gov/manage/h2a.
14. "H-2A Guestworker Program," Farmworker Justice, January 29, 2021, https://www.farmworkerjustice.org/advocacy_program/h-2a-guestworker-program/.
15. "Making an Impact," Farmworkerjustice.org, 2017, http://www.farmworkerjustice.org/wp-content/uploads/2012/04/FarmworkerJustice-Brochure_0.pdf.
16. "Astronaut José M. Hernández," José M. Hernández Reaching for the Stars Foundation, January 29, 2021, http://astrojh.org/astronaut-jose-m-hernandez.
17. "Guiding Principles for Dual Language Education—Third Edition," Center for Applied Linguistics, Dual Language Education of New Mexico and Santillana USA, January 29, 2021, https://www.cal.org/resource-center/publications-products/guiding-principles-3.
18. V. P. Collier and W. P. Thomas, "Validating the power of bilingual schooling: Thirty-two years of large-scale, longitudinal research," *Annual Review of Applied Linguistics* 37 (2017): 1–15.
19. "MTTS: A System of Supports That Works," Illinois MTTS Network Multi-Tiered System of Supports, 2018, https://ilmtss.net.
20. "Long-Term English Learners: Spotlight on an Overlooked Population," Regional Educational Laboratory West at WestEd, January 29, 2021, https://www.wested.org/resources/long-term-english-learner-students/.
21. "Migrant Education—Basic State Formula Grants," Office of Migrant Education, US Department of Education, January 29, 2021, https://www2.ed.gov/programs/mep/index.html.
22. "Why Don't Immigrants Apply for Citizenship? There Is No Line for Many Unauthorized Immigrants," American Immigration Council, November 2019, https://www.americanimmigrationcouncil.org/sites/default/files/research/why_dont_immigrants_apply_for_citizenship.pdf.

Chapter 4

1. "Vietnam," The World Factbook, Central Intelligence Agency, January 4, 2021, https://www.cia.gov/the-world-factbook/countries/vietnam/.
2. Elijah Alperin and Jeanne Batalova, "Vietnamese Immigrants in the United States," Migration Policy Institute, September 13, 2018, https://www.migrationpolicy.org/article/vietnamese-immigrants-united-states-5.
3. Vietnamese population in the US, 2000–2015, Pew Research Center, January 4, 2021, https://www.pewsocialtrends.org/fact-sheet/asian-americans-vietnamese-in-the-u-s-fact-sheet/.
4. Asian Americans, Pew Research Center, January 4, 2021, https://www.pewresearch.org/topics/asian-americans/.
5. Gustavo López, Neil G. Ruiz, and Eileen Patten, "Key facts about Asian Americans, a diverse and growing population," Pew Research Center, September 8, 2017, https://www.pewresearch.org/fact-tank/2017/09/08/key-facts-about-asian-americans/.
6. Viet Thanh Nguyen, "Asian Americans Are Still Caught in the Trap of the 'Model Minority' Stereotype. And It Creates Inequality for All," *Time*, June 26, 2020, https://time.com/5859206/anti-asian-racism-america/.

7. Family of US Citizens, US Citizenship and Immigration Services, March 23, 2020, https://www.uscis.gov/family/family-of-us-citizens.
8. Martin R. West and Guido Schwerdt, "The Middle School Plunge," *Education Next*, 2021, http://educationnext.org/the-middle-school-plunge/.
9. Executive Summary of Research on Middle School Configuration, Edmonds, January 4, 2021, https://www.edmonds.wednet.edu/UserFiles/Servers/Server_306670/Image/Community/Middle%20School%20Configurations/Executive%20Summary%20of%20Research%20on%20Middle%20School%20Configuration%20(1).pdf.
10. Marshall Terrill, "Education professor brings landmark research project with him to ASU; work focuses on making transition to middle school less painful," Arizona State University, October 9, 2020, https://asunow.asu.edu/20201009-discoveries-simple-intervention-strategy-improves-outcomes-middle-school-students.
11. Joyce W. Nutta et al., *Educating English Learners: What Every Classroom Teacher Needs to Know* (Cambridge, MA: Harvard Education Press, 2014).
12. National Achievement-Level Results, The Nation's Report Card, January 4, 2021, https://www.nationsreportcard.gov/reading/nation/achievement/?grade=8.
13. "Long-term English learner students: Spotlight on an overlooked population," REL West, November 2016, https://www.wested.org/wp-content/uploads/2016/11/LTEL-factsheet.pdf.
14. Claude Goldenberg, "Teaching English Language Learners, What the Research Does—and Does Not—Say," *American Educator*, Summer 2008, https://www.aft.org/sites/default/files/periodicals/goldenberg.pdf.
15. Joyce W. Nutta et al., *Show, Tell, Build: Twenty Key Instructional Tools and Techniques for Educating English Learners* (Cambridge: Harvard Education Press, 2018).
16. My Name, My Identity, Santa Clara County Office of Education, January 4, 2021, https://www.mynamemyidentity.org/.

Chapter 5

1. As became apparent in the Rebez family's first outing in Tyler, turning right on a red light isn't permitted in Iraq.
2. "Iraq," The World Factbook, Central Intelligence Agency, January 4, 2021, https://www.cia.gov/the-world-factbook/static/94a7ec6aa19b832baabc1948422fb9cf/IZ-summary.pdf.
3. "Iraq Education," IRFAD, January 4, 2021, http://www.irfad.org/iraq-education/.
4. Besheer Mohamed, "Who are the Iraqi Kurds?," Pew Research Center, August 20, 2014, https://www.pewresearch.org/fact-tank/2014/08/20/who-are-the-iraqi-kurds/.
5. "The World's Muslims: Unity and Diversity," Pew Research Center, August 9, 2012, https://www.pewforum.org/2012/08/09/the-worlds-muslims-unity-and-diversity-executive-summary/#sunnishia.
6. "Who are the Kurds?," BBC, October 15, 2019, https://www.bbc.com/news/world-middle-east-29702440; Erin Blakemore, "Today, the Kurds are spread across four nations. Who are they?," *National Geographic*, August 16, 2019, https://www.nationalgeographic.com/culture/people/reference/who-are-kurds/.
7. "United States Hosts Over 1 Million International Students for the Fifth Consecutive Year," Institute of International Education, Inc., November 16, 2020, https://www.iie.org/en/Why-IIE/Announcements/2020/11/2020-Open-Doors-Report.

8. Mattea Cumoletti and Jeanne Batalova, "Middle Eastern and North African Immigrants in the United States," Migration Policy Institute, January 10, 2018, https://www.migrationpolicy.org/article/middle-eastern-and-north-african-immigrants-united-states-2016#Distribution_by_State_and_Key_Cities.
9. Min Huang et al., "High School Graduation Rates Across English Learner Student Subgroups in Arizona," WestEd, January 4, 2021, https://www.wested.org/resources/graduation-rates-across-english-learner-subgroups-in-arizona/#.
10. "Understanding Language, Language, Literacy, and Learning in the Content Areas," Stanford University, January 4, 2021, https://ell.stanford.edu/teaching_resources/math; in *Educating English Learners* and *Show, Tell, Build*, my coauthors and I provide resources for sentence frames and word banks.
11. Joyce W. Nutta et al., *Educating English Learners: What Every Classroom Teacher Needs to Know* (Cambridge, MA: Harvard Education Press, 2014).
12. Newcomer Toolkit, US Department of Education, January 4, 2021, https://www2.ed.gov/about/offices/list/oela/newcomers-toolkit/ncomertoolkit.pdf.
13. Dani's accent in English was influenced by Arabic sounds, which have a /b/ phoneme but not a /p/ one, which results in the substitution of the /b/ sound for the /p/ sound in English.

Chapter 6

1. Carnegie units are a standard way of measuring instructional time in US schools. They were established in 1905 to document the amount of time a student spent learning a given subject, with the purpose of determining if a student had accumulated enough hours of study in each subject to be prepared for college. They are still widely used in the US. For more information, see "Carnegie Foundation Releases Results of Two-Year Study on the Carnegie Unit," Carnegie Foundation for the Advancement of Teaching, January 28, 2015, https://www.carnegiefoundation.org/newsroom/news-releases/carnegie-foundation-releases-results-two-year-study-carnegie-unit/.
2. "Ya es Hora.," Familia es Familia, February 7, 2021, https://www.familiaesfamilia.org. "Venezuela," The World Factbook, Central Intelligence Agency, February 7, 2021.
3. https://www.cia.gov/the-world-factbook/static/e4ac1d7f27fc360694b441dd87a788dd/VE-summary.pdf.
4. "Travel Facts," Venezuela, The World Factbook, Central Intelligence Agency, January 28, 2021, https://www.cia.gov/the-world-factbook/static/0d09c7f2d5dbf3be40f407dc79ad3ea6/VE-travel-facts.pdf.
5. Luis Noe-Bustamante, Antonio Flores, and Sono Shah, "Facts on Hispanics of Venezuelan origin in the United States, 2017," Pew Research Center, Hispanic Trends, February 7, 2021, https://www.pewresearch.org/hispanic/fact-sheet/u-s-hispanics-facts-on-venezuelan-origin-latinos/.
6. Jie Zong and Jeanne Batalova, "South American Immigrants in the United States," Migration Policy Institute, November 7, 2017, https://www.migrationpolicy.org/article/south-american-immigrants-united-states-2017.
7. Bustamante et al., "Facts on Hispanics of Venezuelan origin in the United States, 2017."

8. Joyce W. Nutta et al., *Show, Tell, Build: Twenty Key Instructional Tools and Techniques for Educating English Learners* (Cambridge, MA: Harvard Education Press, 2018).
9. "Grading International and ELL Student Writing," UW Writes, Writing Resources for Departments, Teachers, & Students, The Writing Program of the College of Arts and Sciences, University of Washington, February 7, 2021, https://depts.Washington.edu/writeuw/gradingesl.html.
10. Zina Lawrence and Anne Sinkey, "Start the Semester Inclusively," 7 Ways to Set All Students Up for Success on Day One, Harvard Business Publishing Education, January 18, 2021, https://hbsp.harvard.edu/inspiring-minds/7-inclusive-ways-to-set-all-students-up-for-success-on-day-one?cid=email%7Celoqua%7C2021-02-05-inspiring-minds-digest-a%7C734394%7Cinspiringminds%7Ceducator%7Cinspiring-minds-article%7Cfeb20212263&acctID=15158405.
11. Diversity Visa Program, US Department of State—Bureau of Consular Affairs, February 7, 2021, https://travel.state.gov/content/travel/en/us-visas/immigrate/diversity-visa-program-entry/diversity-visa-submit-entry1.html.
12. Cathy Fleischer, "ESL, ELL, Generation 1.5—Why Are These Terms Important?," National Council of Teachers of English, September 7, 2017, https://ncte.org/blog/2017/09/esl-ell-generation-1-5-why-are-these-terms-important/.
13. The idiom *that's a wrap* means that something is finished. It is a term that began in the film industry and then became widely used. It originally meant that the recording was finished and the film was ready for production, as in to *wrap something up* in order to send or give to someone else. Later the term changed into noun form (a wrap).

Conclusion

1. There are numerous free materials for teachers that support antiracist teaching. Some worth exploring are: Tools for Anti-Racist Teaching/PBS Education; Becoming an Anti-Racist Educator/Wheaton College Massachusetts; Learning for Justice/SPLC; Jerry Fingal and Samantha Mack, "9 Resources for Teaching Anti-Racism," International Society for Technology in Education, (ISTE), June 3, 2020, https://www.iste.org/explore/classroom/9-resources-teaching-anti-racism; Hedreich Nichols, "A Guide to Equity and Antiracism for Educators," Edutopia, George Lucas Educational Foundation, June 5, 2020, https://www.edutopia.org/article/guide-equity-and-antiracism-educators.
2. "Proven tools and support to help educators and multilingual learners, World-Class Instructional Design and Assessment (WIDA), February 7, 2021, https://wida.wisc.edu; "The ELP Assessment System," English Language Proficiency Assessments, February 7, 2021, https://www.elpa21.org.
3. Henry A. Giroux, *Teachers as Intellectuals: Toward a Critical Pedagogy of Learning* (Westport, CT: Bergin & Garvey, 1988).
4. Pope Francis, *Laudato Si': On Care for Our Common Home*, Encyclical Letter (Huntington, IN: Our Sunday Visitor, 2015).

ACKNOWLEDGMENTS

MY ENDURING GRATITUDE goes to Caroline Chauncey, who years ago was able to see through my messy compilation of ideas to shape a book that started a series with Harvard Education Press, of which this book is the fourth. I am especially appreciative of the guidance provided by Jayne Fargnoli, whose feedback put wind in my sails and who had an extraordinary affinity for and knowledge of the book's subject. Lucky me that she came into this project unexpectedly! Many thanks, also, to Molly Grab for her helpful editorial comments, Jane Gebhart for her copyediting expertise, Anne Noonan for overseeing the production process, and Laura Godwin for helping the book find those it can benefit.

I am indebted to Carine Feyten for authoring the book's foreword and for the many other gifts she has given me. I would not have the career that has brought me so much joy and fulfillment if not for Dr. Feyten.

My deepest thanks are reserved for my family, which has been a source of ideas and inspiration. Giorgio and Francesca, who read all my drafts and cheered me on; Marco, who discussed the fulfillment and challenges of writing and publishing with me; Mirai, who read stories and contrasted her own EL immigrant story with different characters in the manuscript; Troy, who helped proofread and cheerlead; Betty and Gloria, who shared their pride in my work with others; and Junné, my darling granddaughter, to whom this book is dedicated.

I am so grateful for my lifelong friends, Donna Lawless, who helped me find resources in the endnotes and formatted them all in Streator Style; and Maria Antonietta Robimarga, who sent me *In the Sea There are Crocodiles*, and encouraged me often with emoji-filled texts. I don't know how I got so lucky to have you both in my life.

Many thanks to my colleagues who supported this work in multiple ways. Collaborating with my HEP coauthors Kouider Mokhtari, Edwidge Crevecoeur Bryant, Florin Mihai, and Carine Strebel has elevated my scholarship and instilled a deeper commitment to the principles we share. My UCF colleagues Kerry Purmensky, Marjorie Ceballos, Leslie Mendez, Laura Monroe, Nadia

Garzon, Yvonne Cadiz, Donita Grissom, Linda Rosa-Lugo, Malcolm Butler, and Sissi Carroll helped make this book happen in so many ways, from answering tiny-detail questions about a particular grade level (Leslie) or culture (Kerry) or test (Linda), to covering for me when I needed time to write, and inspiring me with their excellence.

During the writing process, I felt uplifted and informed by many colleagues, students, friends, and teachers who were cultural consultants and/or grade-level experts: Eloy Hernández, so generous in answering every trivial question I asked, and his lovely daughter Sofia; Julie Almeida Snyder, the most altruistic person I know; Lorena Kogan, an amazing dual language teacher; Mais Al-Jabbawi and Abdulmajeed Alotaibi, who helped me get important details right; Maria Vargas, who shared her inspiring story; Lauranette Ramos, who helped me understand middle school; Hong Van Le, with whom I had the privilege to discover commonalities we were unaware of; and Maria Carreras Torrado, whose expertise in early learning and dual language education is remarkable; Rick Hamlin and Jim Hinch for helping me learn how to tell stories; Susan Bubbers for teaching me about the power of parables; and Alex Davies, I miss you and think of you always. May your memory be honored by these stories.

It's fitting to end the book by thanking all my students over the years who weathered the perfect storm of learning English while learning how to live, study, and work in a new country. Your stories inspired these stories, and my wish for the book, and for my continuing work, is to help make life better for English learners from this moment on. For everything I learned from you, I am forever grateful.

ABOUT THE AUTHOR

DR. JOYCE W. NUTTA is professor of World Languages Education and the ESOL Endorsement, Dual Language Education Graduate Certificate, and TESOL PhD Track Coordinator at the University of Central Florida. She is devoted to educating teachers of all subjects and grade levels about English learners and to equipping teachers with tools and techniques that support English learners' academic achievement and language development.

INDEX